"Thomas Søbirk Petersen is a philos
stream thinking by controversial id
As an untiring challenger of con
strated that challenging establisheu
insights. His new book *Doping in Sport* is testame..
— *Verner Møller, Professor in the Departme..*
Public Health, Aarhus University, Denmark

"There are few topics more loaded with hypocrisy, bullshit (in the
sense of saying things with no regard for truth or falsity), implicit and
politically correct assumptions never justified, than in the discussion
about doping in sport. This book is different. With the author's analyt-
ical rigor and sharp eye at all the contradictory views, it prepares the
way for critical and systematic thoughts about the subject. I congratu-
late the author for having had the courage to write this timely book. It
was a pleasure to read it."
— *Torbjörn Tännsjö, Professor of Practical*
Philosophy, Stockholm University, Sweden

"Analysing the most widespread colloquial and scholarly arguments
for banning doping, Thomas Søbirk Petersen provides a passionate
and thought-provoking defense of the need to include pro-doping
voices in the debate on whether the World Anti-Doping Agency should
allow performance-enhancing substances and methods."
— *Francisco Javier Lopez Frias, Assistant*
Professor, Health and Human Development,
Pennsylvania State University, USA

Doping in Sport

In this provocative and thought-provoking book, Professor of Ethics Thomas Søbirk Petersen explains why the World Anti-Doping Agency's doping rules are poorly justified and makes a case for a new third way in anti-doping policy that would allow athletes to use substances and methods currently on WADA's prohibited list.

The book identifies, clarifies and challenges the central arguments that are used in the often highly emotional debates around doping, and argues strongly that open dialogue about doping is essential as it defines the territory in which athletes, physicians, managers, coaches and pharmaceutical companies can operate safely. It is rooted in the theory of ethics and illustrated with real cases, examples and experiences from sport at all levels, from the auto-biographical to some of the most high-profile doping cases in history.

This is an essential addition to the bookshelves of researchers and students of sports studies like sports philosophy, sports law, sports medicine and the sociology of sport, and a fascinating read for anybody interested in the darker side of sport and in its possible futures.

Thomas Søbirk Petersen is Professor of Ethics at Roskilde University, Department of Communication and Arts, Denmark. Besides having won over 20 Danish tennis championships, he has participated in the French Open as a junior, and is Nordic champion in tennis for +50 veteran teams.

Routledge Focus on Sport, Culture and Society

Routledge Focus on Sport, Culture and Society showcases the latest cutting-edge research in the sociology of sport and exercise. Concise in form (20,000–50,000 words) and published quickly (within three months), the books in this series represents an important channel through which authors can disseminate their research swiftly and make an impact on current debates. We welcome submissions on any topic within the socio-cultural study of sport and exercise, including but not limited to subjects such as gender, race, sexuality, disability, politics, the media, social theory, Olympic Studies, and the ethics and philosophy of sport. The series aims to be theoretically-informed, empirically-grounded and international in reach, and will include a diversity of methodological approaches.

List of titles

For more information about this series, please visit: https://www.routledge.com/sport/series/RFSCS

Doping in Sport
A Defence

Thomas Søbirk Petersen

Routledge
Taylor & Francis Group

LONDON AND NEW YORK

First published 2021
by Routledge
2 Park Square, Milton Park, Abingdon, Oxon OX14 4RN

and by Routledge
605 Third Avenue, New York, NY 10017

First issued in paperback 2022

Routledge is an imprint of the Taylor & Francis Group, an informa business

Copyright © 2021 Thomas Søbirk Petersen

Publisher's Note
The publisher has gone to great lengths to ensure the quality of this reprint but points out that some imperfections in the original copies may be apparent.

British Library Cataloguing-in-Publication Data
A catalogue record for this book is available from the British Library

Library of Congress Cataloging-in-Publication Data
Names: Petersen, Thomas S. (Thomas Søbirk), author.
Title: Doping in sport: a defence / Thomas Søbirk Petersen.
Description: Abingdon, Oxon; New York, NY: Routledge, 2021. |
Series: Routledge focus on sport, culture and society |
Includes bibliographical references and index. |
Identifiers: LCCN 2020018940 | ISBN 9780367528300 (hardback) |
ISBN 9781003058564 (ebook)
Subjects: LCSH: Doping in sports—Moral and ethical
aspects. | Sports medicine—Moral and ethical aspects.
Classification: LCC RC1230 .P4786 2021 | DDC 362.29088/796—dc23
LC record available at https://lccn.loc.gov/2020018940

ISBN 13: 978-0-367-52831-7 (pbk)
ISBN 13: 978-0-367-52830-0 (hbk)
ISBN 13: 978-1-00-305856-4 (ebk)

DOI: 10.4324/9781003058564

Typeset in Times New Roman
by codeMantra

Contents

Preface

Pregame: from doped tennis player to professor of ethics

I'm doped. I just don't know it. I'm totally baked on weed. In many ways, it's a problem for me. It is especially a problem because I'm on a tennis court playing the quarterfinals at the Danish tennis championships. I'm playing men's doubles with my partner and team mate Simon Bastiansen. We are playing on Copenhagen Tennis Club's (KB) old indoor tennis court against tennis legend Jørgen Ulrich[1] and his son Stein Ulrich. We are at the beginning of the 1980s and my career as a young tennis player is starting to look promising. I've been selected for the Danish Davis Cup team in tennis, I'm Danish national champion for juniors, part of KB's elite division team and will soon be participating in the junior tournament at the prestigious Grand Slam tournament French Open.

Simon and I did not play particularly well since the joint I had smoked did nothing to enhance my game on the court, quite the opposite. I felt my heart pounding, shifted between states of being partly paranoid and inappropriately goofy, my judgement of distance was much worse than normal and I was close to having a monstrous anxiety attack. Shortly after the match, I had another go at smoking a joint but suffered a massive anxiety attack. So now, I haven't smoked a joint in 35 years. Though I wouldn't mind at all playing against a tennis player who was stoned, as it would only increase my chances of winning considerably. Being stoned on weed is definitely not something I would recommend. After my wild and rebellious youth, I now prefer being buzzed on alcohol over being baked on weed at parties.

But back to the tennis match. To my recollection, and our recollection is something all athletes care a lot about and why we hardly ever forget our results (especially when we win), we just scraped through and won the match. Thanks Simon! The end of the story, which is worth mentioning, is that I was not the only one of the four double players who smoked that day. Jørgen Ulrich also smoked a lot. Remember, at that time, smokers were not frowned upon. Forty-eight-year old Jørgen Ulrich smoked a cigarette on the way from the locker room to the court. And to my and Simon's surprise, he put out the cigarette on the net post on the court. After this macho move, Mr Ulrich looked at Simon and I and calmly asked us while blowing smoke in our faces: "So, boys, are you ready to play?"

It was not until later in life that I discovered that I had used a substance in the match which both then and today is prohibited to use in sports. So I was not just a stoned tennis player, but also a doped tennis player. But I can honestly say – like the former winners of Tour de France, Lance Armstrong and Bjarne Riis – that I have never been tested positive for doping. However, it is part of my story that, contrary to Lance and Bjarne, I have never actually been tested for doping. That is a fact even though I have played on all Danish national tennis teams from a very young age to above 50 and participated in numerous national and international championships and other tournaments in Denmark and abroad. However, contrary to the use of weed, most types of doping can be performance enhancing in terms of endurance, speed, concentration and building muscle.

My own experience with doping got me thinking at a young age whether we have the best doping rules. Why is cannabis on the prohibited list when smoke on the brain typically makes an athlete perform poorly? If you and I want to perform better at a party or in other social contexts, we can drink alcohol to get into a good mood and become more extrovert. And if you want to relax, you can smoke tobacco, and if you need a boost you can have some coffee or an energy drink. Yet, despite the fact that both alcohol and tobacco cause hundreds of thousands of deaths each year in the USA and the UK alone, both are still allowed. So why prohibit adult athletes from using drugs regardless of whether they enhance their performance or, as in the case of cannabis, deteriorate their performance. Athletes (and all others) have always used performance-enhancing drugs and there is every indication that quite a limited number of people have died from doping in the approximately 3,000-year history of sports.[2]

I for one have for many years wondered why doping is illegal in the world of sports, and my wonder has only intensified after becoming professor of the philosophical subject of ethics. This wonder has made me write a book that combines two of my greatest passions in life – sports and philosophy.

The purpose of this book is to identify, clarify and challenge some of the central arguments that are used in the often extremely emotional debate that primarily focusses on rejecting the use of doping. It is my hope that by providing an overview of the arguments – and by identifying some of the challenges to the various arguments in the debate – I can help improve our decision basis in relation to the extent to which doping should be a punishable offence in the world of sports. Both for those who do *not* have a fixed opinion in the area and for anti-dopers or pro-dopers, who want an overview of the central viewpoints in the doping debate. I further hope that my effort to clarify and challenge the arguments will help cultivate a productive dialogue where all arguments are given a *fair trial* instead of the prevailing one-sided condemnation of doping. An open dialogue about doping is important since the question of where the line should be drawn when it comes to doping in sports is highly relevant in terms of the scope within which athletes, sports physicians, sports managers, coaches and pharmaceutical companies can operate in the world of sports.

Notes

1 Jørgen Ulrich (1935–2010) won more than 40 Danish national tennis championships and participated 21 times at Wimbledon.
2 Møller (2010, pp. 32–48).

Acknowledgements

Good game

When a tennis match is over, it is good form that the players shake hands and say "Good game". One of the reasons for this is that it is impossible to play a game and test and improve your own game without an opponent/player on the other side of the net. You can say something similar about my work on this book. I would not have been able to write this book or get through the struggle it sometimes is to write a book had it not been for other people who served as my sounding board. I would therefore like to thank a number of persons and organisations for helping me write this book.

It would like to start by expressing my gratitude to my Danish colleagues in moral philosophy at Roskilde University Jesper Ryberg, Sune Lægaard, Fatima Sabir, Frej Klem Thomsen, Søren Sofus Wichmann and Rune Klingenberg. They have all contributed with spirited and critical talks over the years about the ethical concerns of using doping in the world of sports. A special thanks goes to Jesper Ryberg and Kasper Lippert-Rasmussen for many fruitful discussions. I would also like to express my thanks to my foreign colleagues Julian Savulescu, Claudio Tamburrini, Torbjörn Tännsjö, Bengt Kayser, Paul Dimeo and Andy Miah, who are all part of the small crowd of moral philosophers who are 'pro-dopers' or at least very critical of the current anti-doping policy. Although I do not always agree with these six scholars, my talks with them at conferences and seminars as well as their written research have given me the motivation to write this book. My thanks also go out to the many students at Roskilde University who have written about "Ethics and doping" in papers and bachelor projects. Your fresh perspective, curiosity and questions have been a constant reminder that this topic is not just relevant from an academic perspective, but also from a personal and societal perspective. I would also like to thank some of the institutions that have invited me to present and discuss my research on ethics and doping. Thanks to Cambridge University, University of Copenhagen, Aarhus University and Aalborg University and all those who attended for your good observations and comments. Also thanks to Associate Professor of Sports Science at Aarhus University, Ask Vest Christiansen, who have read and commented my first and early attempts at criticising the current doping policy. I would also like to thank Professor of Sports Science at Aarhus University, Verner Møller, for inspiration and conversations in connection with the writing of this book. My thanks also go out to Roskilde University, whose management have supported me in my work. In this respect, I particularly think of our Rector, Hanne Leth Andersen, and our former Head of Department, Hanne Løngren and our current Head, Julie Sommerlund. Thanks to my old tennis partner, Simon Bastiansen, for helping me remember how things played out. As a side benefit, my work on this book has brought us back together after almost 25 years. Thanks also to my sister, Pia Bech, for proofreading and commenting on the early drafts of a first version of the book – which was published in Danish in 2018 (this book is a much improved version of the publication in Danish). Thanks to Anti Doping Danmark for answering many of my questions. Thanks also to Routledge and editors Simon Whitmore and Rebecca Connor for your support and belief in the book project *Doping in Sport: A Defence*. Finally, I would like to express my thanks to my family, Helle, Amanda and Malthe for being the best travel companions through life.

Warm up
The tunnel vision of the doping debate

Let's, as is common for athletes, warm up to the topic *Ethics and doping* with some imaginative visualisations. Imagine Chris Froome winning the Tour de France in 2021 because he completed the stages of the Tour with a microscopic auxiliary engine on his racer. Alternatively, that the American swimmer and five times Olympic champion Katie Ledecky in impressive style scooped a lot of medals in swimming at the Tokyo 2021 Olympics because she wore webbed transparent gloves. If these visualisations were realised in the real world, most would think that Chris Froome and Katie Ledecky had acted unethically. Unethically because they both had used aids that are banned. People would probably have the same attitude if an athlete in violation of the doping rules uses performance-enhancing drugs such as anabolic-androgenic steroids (AAS) or erythropoietin (EPO) in their effort to win.

When Lance Armstrong cycled out of the closet in 2013 and answered *Yes* to the infamous question by TV host Oprah Winfrey, "Did you ever take banned drugs to enhance your performance?", the public indignation and criticism were staggering. Lances' colleagues on the road, like Tyler Hamilton, Eric Zabel, Johan Museeuw and Bjarne Riis, faced the same condemnation. They have all had to throw in the towel and in time admit that they have used doping during their career.

When alcoholised archers, racing cyclists on EPO, synchronised swimmers intoxicated on glitter and pot and race horses on Viagra break the doping rules, it is generally morally wrong. And when a democratically elected sports federation or anti-doping organisation has established some common rules that the athletes should follow, it is in principle morally wrong to break the rules. That is one of the reasons why sports associations punish athletes who are tested positive with suspension, condemnation and possibly by stripping them of their prize money, records and medals.

But even if it is generally wrong to break the rules in sports, the rules are not carved in stone. And, more importantly, it could be argued that the current doping rules are morally unfair or that the rules are enforced in an unfair way, e.g. because the rules are not harmonised all over the world,[1] and that we should therefore moderate our indignation towards athletes who are tested for using doping. In the world of sports, as in all other areas, most rules or codes of practice are up for discussion. It used to be legal to sell, buy and abuse slaves. But although it was once legal to keep slaves, we would characterise the law as morally wrong today. The world of sports offers many examples of rules being changed over time. For instance, the diameter of the official table tennis ball was changed from 38 to 40 millimetres in 2000. The purpose was to reduce the speed of the game so that the rallies would become longer and thus more audience-friendly. Other examples of changing the rules in sports include women being allowed to participate in marathon races (since the 1984 Olympic Games) and pole vault (since the 2000 Olympic Games).

The same has happened within doping. Rules constantly change. For instance, caffeine was taken off the World Anti-Doping Agency's (WADA) list of prohibited substances in 2004. However, the use of certain substances and methods only constitute cheating and are thus immoral to use in sports as long as they are listed on WADA's prohibited list. It is hopefully clear by now that I believe that there is room to improve the current doping rules. I believe that it should be allowed to use a wide range of substances and methods that can currently be found on WADA's prohibited list. I will spend most of this book elaborating this view. But first a brief comment on why the critical voice in the doping debate is under pressure. Basically, it is a bit strange that we in many parts of the world can have a fair and open discussion whether, e.g. cannabis or assisted suicide should be legalised, or whether prostitution should be or remain legal, when we are practically not allowed to discuss whether doping should be allowed in the world of sports.

I think that it is a problem that criticism of the current doping rules is practically absent in the public and sports-policy debate, apart from the infrequent critical voices of a handful of scholars. In most parts of the world, the doping debate is characterised by an extreme tunnel vision since all athletes, politicians and sports managers who have public airtime express that doping is bad or the invention of the devil. However, when sports associations punish athletes who use doping, most would agree with me that we should at least demand being given a good reason for why the use of doping is so immoral that it should lead to punishment. It is not enough simply to argue that doping is contrary to the rules. Instead, it should be considered whether there are any good reasons to accept rules that lead to punishment. A punishment that might mean that athletes, besides loosing their job and being stripped of prize money, rankings, records and medals, might also loose central parts of their identity and social network. Further, the convicted doping user may be and is commonly exposed, stigmatised, ridiculed and condemned in the pillory of public media. Punishing athletes for using doping not only affects the athlete in negative ways, but may also come at a huge price for the athlete's family and friends.

The doping rules are also relevant in respect of what drugs sports physicians may legally prescribe to the athletes. The drugs on the prohibited list are also relevant to what drugs pharmaceutical companies might choose to produce and sell to athletes. Therefore, it goes without saying that the substances and methods that are illegal for athletes to use restrict the opportunities of a large number of individuals and organisations.

The opportunities of using doping raise various ethical questions: Is WADA's current prohibition against doping morally acceptable? Should the use of doping be illegal under state legislation? How hard and how should athletes who use doping be punished? Is it ethically acceptable to test athletes for the use of doping 24/7 and, e.g. test them the night before an important competition? Is it fair that athletes should always inform WADA of their whereabouts? Should an entire team (e.g. a football team) be collectively punished if one player on the team uses doping without the others knowing? Should referees be allowed to dope and enhance their performance in order to increase fair play on the pitch?[2] Although all these questions are central and important – and to some extent are related – this book will focus on the first question. In other words a critical discussion of various answers to the question: Is WADA's current prohibition against doping morally acceptable?

The tunnel vision of the international debate on doping can be explained in many ways. However, it is clear that the fact that it may have severe personal repercussions for athletes and sports physicians to speak publicly and negatively about the current doping rules serves as a strong damper on a critical and nuanced public dialogue. If an athlete, sports physician, coach or sports manager voices criticism of the current doping rules, it may result in losing sponsors, work, networks and friends. Indeed, it comes at a heavy price for particularly people in the sports world to speak critically about doping. Imagine if a former racing cyclist like Lance Armstrong spoke positively about doping and said: "It's fantastic and not harmful at all – quite the opposite – as long as you are assisted by a professional physician and follow her advice"?! If Lance Armstrong challenged the opinion makers in this way, he would unlikely be able to keep his job as a sports commentator and would probably also fall in public esteem. However, it is a problem that many of the people who know something about doping in practice cannot speak publicly and critically about the doping rules without having to pay a huge price.

It is essential that we have a critical public and political debate about doping. Because, as we have seen, the current doping policy has a massive impact on people's lives. Not just the athletes and their families. The current doping policy also greatly impacts on the moral and legal scope within which sports physicians, coaches, sports managers and pharmaceutical companies can operate. Moreover, and equally important, the current doping policy has also resulted in, e.g. Russia being banned from a host of international sports events because they have systematically been cheating with doping tests in favour of Russian athletes. This ban can easily have a negative effect on international politics and diplomacy between Russia and other countries. So whether doping is banned. or not might also have consequences on an international scale.

I believe that it is a scientific and democratic problem that those who know something about doping and want to criticise the current doping policy are given no real voice in the debate. With this book, I want to give a voice to the critics of the official and current doping policy. You may argue that any use of doping is obviously wrong, and claim like the former head of WADA, Dick Pound, "Doping is bad, period".[3] That is not my position. But before well-intentioned sports journalists, sports managers and politicians get too high on their moral horse by arguing that use of doping is 'unforgivable' or 'insane' or 'bad, period', let us instead try to investigate whether the rationale for the current doping policy builds on clear concepts, objective knowledge and a solid ethical foundation.

The dream of the clean sport

The tunnel vision in the debate on doping is mainly caused by the dream of a doping-free sport. A dream that has only grown stronger since the introduction of the doping policy in the mid-1960s. Just consider what WADA considers its mission: "WADA's mission is to lead a collaborative worldwide movement for doping-free sport".[4]

I believe that the dream of a doping-free or so-called clean sport is only a dream and will never be anything but a dream. A dream world made of young, healthy, athletic and smiling athletes that we only now and then see depicted in propagandist, glossy pictures from sports parades in totalitarian regimes. There are several reasons why a clean, doping-free sport is an illusion.

First, doping is efficient in terms of enhancing the athletes' performance. For instance, even at low doses, anabolic steroids are capable of increasing muscle mass and the energy output of racing cyclists by 5–20%[5] and increase endurance by as much as 10%.[6] So for athletes seeking the glory of victory – fame, money or big muscles – it will always be very tempting to use doping.

Second, the risk of being tested positive is not particularly big. Numbers from major international competitions show that a mere 10–28% of athletes have been tested, and the number is considerably lower in minor competitions. Furthermore, the number of athletes being tested outside competition is even lower and practically non-existent in some sports.[7] Some recent research also shows that between 40 and 75% of athletes at major events such as the World Athletics Championships have used doping at least once within the past 12 months.[8] Other research concerning the prevalence of doping use among elite athletes shows us that it is consistently used at least once a year by over 20% of the athletes.[9]

Third, even if a doping user is picked out for testing, they will almost always be one step ahead of the doping inspectors and the doping labs. The athletes are one up on the inspectors as no reliable tests exist to reveal the use of certain doping drugs and methods.[10] This applies to certain types of growth hormone and insulin with a very short half-life and which are therefore only traceable in the body for a few hours after being absorbed by the body.[11] Most elite athletes and their doctors know how to use doping in order to avoid getting caught.

For example, the Danish cyclist Michael Rasmussen has described how it is practically impossible to get caught for using blood doping if you draw small amounts of your own blood and supplement the reinjection of blood with saline injections.[12] Changes in the athlete's haematocrit level[13] will therefore not stand out and will drop within the natural variation in the athlete's normal haematocrit level. Another example supporting this observation is the story about the cycling phenomenon Lance Armstrong. According to the International Cycling Union (UCI) and the US Anti-Doping Agency (USADA), Lance Armstrong was tested for use of doping approximately 280 times.[14] Yet, Armstrong was never tested positive. Some sports researchers also support the claim that it is mainly the careless or unintelligent riders that are caught as users of performance-enhancing drugs.[15] The fact that Lance Armstrong was exposed as a doping user some eight years after his active career had ended was not the result of a positive doping test. Rather, it was because his former team mates Floyd Landis and Tyler Hamilton (and others) delivered testimonies against Armstrong and stated that they had seen Armstrong use doping.

What is doping?

Before we get started, it would be appropriate to explain how I use the word 'doping' in the following. Doping can be defined in different ways.[16] However, in the following, I use the word 'doping' to describe that an athlete uses substances or methods on the World Anti-Doping Agency's prohibited list.[17] Since 2004, WADA has published an annual, updated list of prohibited substances and methods.[18] The list includes a number of *performance enhancing* drugs such as amphetamine, anabolic-androgenic steroids (AAS), growth hormones and EPO. However, drugs or substances like alcohol, diuretics (capable of blurring any trace of performance-enhancing drugs and methods) and cannabis, which is typically *not* performance enhancing when used in sports, are also on the prohibited list. But besides drugs, the list also features *methods* such as use of intravenous drip or blood doping. In connection with blood doping, you typically draw 500 ml of blood from the athlete well in advance of a competition and isolate the red blood cells. Just before the competition when the athlete has regenerated the volume of blood drawn, the previously drawn red blood cells will be reinjected (transfused) in the athlete. This supplement means that the athlete will have a higher number of red blood cells. A higher number of red blood cells are able to transport more oxygen to the muscles and will therefore increase the athlete's endurance compared to before the transfusion.

A new doping policy

With this book, I wish to promote a very different doping policy than the one pursued by WADA. WADA is an exponent of a strict doping policy that is essentially very sceptical of the use of pharmaceutical drugs and methods in sports, many of which have become banned to use. WADA's prohibited list includes approximately 300 different substances and methods.[19]

In opposition to WADA's policy, we find representatives of a laissez-faire or permissive attitude to doping. One of the most notorious proponents of a laissez-faire attitude to doping is the Argentinian/Swedish philosopher Claudio Tamburrini. Tamburrini believes that as long as athletes are autonomous individuals then they should be allowed do decide what they want to expose their bodies to. The state, sports associations or others should not decide what a well-informed and rational athlete wants to do with his/her body.[20] Although I cannot subscribe to the laissez-faire attitude to doping, I will apply this perspective to some extent and argue that it should be allowed to use, e.g. EPO, growth hormone, anabolic steroids as well as cannabis and use intravenous injection (of, e.g. water, salt, sugar and vitamins) and blood doping within certain safety limits.[21]

However, in contrast to the laissez-faire strategy, I believe that there are good reasons for continuing prohibiting drugs and substances like alcohol, LSD and cannabis in, e.g. motor racing, platform diving and sailing. And they should remain prohibited as it is extremely dangerous for the athletes and others if they participate at, e.g. a motor race under the influence of alcohol, LSD or cannabis. I also believe that the most recent type of doping, i.e. gene doping, should remain prohibited as its health consequences are highly uncertain. Gene doping, which is in the early stages of development,[22] may, for instance, involve genetic modification of an athlete's blood cells so that the athlete gets a high and permanent haematocrit level without the use of EPO or altitude training.[23] In one area, my position is in fact consistent with that of the legislation of several countries,[24] e.g. Danish and UK legislation. According to Danish and UK legislation, it is not illegal to be doped even if it is illegal to produce, distribute and buy and sell doping, except for those who hold a licence.[25] An athlete who is revealed as a doping user is not punished by the Danish state or by the state of Britain.[26] Instead, athletes who are exposed are instead punished by a parallel penal system mainly governed by the regulations within sports.

Doping is here to stay and we should deal with this fact by aiming for a new approach. A new, or third, approach, which falls between the lines of WADA's fright of drugs and the jungle law of the laissez-faire strategy.

First, we should accept that anyone in their right mind or, in other words, who are rational decision-makers and over the age of 18 can have prescribed performance-enhancing drugs like anabolic steroids, EPO and growth hormone by a physician. This reduces the risk of children under the age of 18 being forced to use doping by their parents and sports managers. Whether you want to use doping must be something you decide yourself but only once you are an adult and a rational decision-maker.

Second, as neither I nor anyone else wants athletes to die, we must to the extent possible ensure that it is not particularly harmful to use doping. In any case, not more harmful than sport already is. For it is no secret that some sports like boxing, motor sport, horse riding, rugby, American football, etc., claim several lives every year. And when it comes to injuries, sport is often extremely harmful. For instance, the injury percentage per season for elite football players is between 70 and 90%[27] and among elite cyclists, 25% should expect to be hospitalised once per season due to crashes and accidents on the roads.[28] We must strive to reduce these horrible numbers, which hold much tragedy. So in connection with lifting the ban on certain doping drugs, I therefore believe that we must put a cap on how much doping a physician can prescribe to his patients. We must define some clear safety values in respect of how much of a performance-enhancing drug you are allowed to use. This might be safety values that clearly indicate when a certain amount of anabolic steroids in the body is harmful. Or we should introduce some threshold values for the haematocrit level of athletes, which the athletes can increase by means of EPO.

We should therefore have some guidelines that define limits for how much of a drug or substance the athletes can use. The athletes should therefore undergo regular testing and they should not be allowed to participate in competitions if they have been tested positive for exceeding the safety values. The International Cycling Union (UCI) did show the way for this strategy when they tested whether the riders have a haematocrit level over 50% before major races. If a rider's level is above 50%, their blood is too thick and they have a much higher risk of developing blood clots. The riders who are tested positive will not be allowed to participate in the competition. The reason is that the riders are regarded as being ill and are therefore suspended from cycling for two weeks.[29] The safety value of 50% applies regardless of whether the reason for a high haematocrit level is use of EPO, oxygen tents or altitude training. WADA do sometimes apply the same kind of strategy when they, e.g. allow athletes to use the asthma medicine salbutamol when it is inhaled at a dose under 1,600 micrograms over 24 hours.

Third, the athletes must receive information from medical experts about various effects and side-effects of using a drug or a method. Finally, access to and administration of doping must take place via a sports physician, who must also regularly monitor the health of the athletes who use doping.

When I present my viewpoint in conversations, research seminars and lectures, I am often told that it will do nothing to change the problems seen in connection with doping today. People will still cheat, even if more drugs or the use of drugs within certain safety limits become allowed to use. Either by using too much of a drug or by using banned drugs. People will still get harmed by using doping and, in respect of the proposed safety values, control and administration would still have to be in place for performing testing and giving suspension. These challenges will naturally still exist – they will probably always exist regardless of the doping policy pursued. Unless laissez-faire is accepted, then cheating concerning doping use will of course not exist. However, my proposal will allow athletes and sports physicians greater scope to use and suggest use of performance-enhancing drugs. Second, my proposal for a new doping policy will mean abandoning a policy that punishes athletes who break the rules. Instead we should favour a policy that strives to protect their health by giving them a short suspension for like one month (or what is necessary to secure health) if they break the doping rules and inform them about how to stay healthy while using drugs.

Some clarifications

Before we embark on a more systematic criticism of the current doping policy, I ask you the readers to keep the following five clarifications in mind.

First, I hope that I have made it clear that I am not a proponent of a laissez-faire attitude to doping – i.e. where all athletes have free access to using any drugs. The title of the book *Doping in Sport: A Defence* might therefore be a bit misleading. However, I mean a defence of doping in the sense that some types of doping which are currently prohibited should be allowed to use.

Second, it should be clear that I do not want to encourage people to use doping if it is allowed. People need to make that decision themselves.

Third, it is important to emphasise that the focus of this book is an ethical analysis of answers to the specific ethical question: Is WADA's prohibition against doping morally acceptable? An ethical analysis implies identifying, reconstructing and systematically criticising the various ethical arguments that are used in the public and scientific doping policy debate. When I, as a moral philosopher, engage in a critical analysis of the ethical arguments in the doping debate, I am of course aware that the arguments often contain pharmaceutical and historical facts. This may be facts that describe when doping use is harmful or how athletes have used doping over the years. When we discuss arguments for and against the current doping policy, these facts naturally need to be as objective as possible. However, the arguments largely also contain reasoning that builds on ethical values.

That might be ethical values that concern respect for autonomy and the spirit of sport and that we should protect the athletes' health. These ethical values, which help guide and justify our behaviour, not only reflect a social reality but are also formulated into concepts that can be ascribed very different meanings. The above-mentioned ethical values are values, to which most would attach importance in an ethical discussion. However, there might also be a great difference in opinion as to how we should balance these values in relation to each other. Should we for instance allow the athletes' right to autonomy (self-determination) to trump the concern for their health? However, the way in which we understand these values and the importance we attach to them are decisive for our position on the extent to which doping should be banned.

Fourth, the scientific/academic literature on ethics and doping has produced no book with the same ambition as this book. Among the texts that I know of, particularly four stands out. Namely, Verner Møller's excellent book *The Ethics of Doping and Anti-doping: Redeeming the Soul of Sport?* (2010). Claudio Tamburrini and Torbjörn Tännsjö's equally excellent anthology *Values in Sport: Elitism, Nationalism, Gender Equality and the Scientific Manufacture of Winners* (2000). Dimeno and Møller's inspiring book *The Anti-Doping Crisis in Sport* (2018) and Jason Mazanov's equally inspiring book *Managing Drugs* (2017). Each of these books dedicates chapters that clearly presents and criticises some of the central arguments against using doping in sport. However, this book differs from the four texts in two key areas. First, I put the cards on the table and argue straight out and at book length that the WADA current doping rules are often poorly justified and that we should let athletes use a broad number of the substances and methods that can be found on WADA's prohibited list. Second, I describe and criticise the arguments that are often put forward in the debate but that are neither presented nor discussed in detail in the above-mentioned books.

Fifth, it is worth noting that the purpose of my criticism of WADA is not to send WADA and other anti-doping agencies off the court. Their work is in many areas legitimate and valuable. They should focus on testing to secure that safety limits have been followed. And, WADA's educational work should be less propagandistic and focus on the science at hand and focus on safety limits and the extremely dangerous use of substances (such as alcohol and cannabis in motor sports) and dangerous methods such as gene doping.

Finally, it is worth noting that when I use the word 'athlete' I not only refer to people who participate in sports competitions. By 'athlete'

I also mean people who do not participate in an official competition against others. Such an athlete might be a person who goes to the gym or is a member of a gymnastics association.

Order of play

Besides the short Pregame and the introductory Warm up, this book consists of seven chapters. Chapter 1 deals with a central argument in the debate: That doping should be banned because it is harmful. However, as I intend to point out, the debate is practically devoid of the argument that allowing various doping drugs can have a beneficial effect on the athletes' health compared to the current prohibition. Particularly if the use of doping is distributed and monitored by physicians and if the use falls within certain health-related safety limits. However, one thing is the extent to which doping is harmful (which is a scientific matter), another is the extent to which we are willing to accept that doping can be harmful (which is an ethical matter).

I will argue that even if doping use can be harmful, then it is not a good enough reason to prohibit doping. We already accept that doing sports can be harmful anyway. Just think of professional boxing, horse riding, motor sports and American football. And we already accept that adults can use tobacco and alcohol. Stimulants that cause thousands of deaths each year. Yet if you accept that sports, alcohol consumption and smoking tobacco are legal, even if they kill thousands, it seems like a double standard to not be willing to accept doping.

In Chapter 2, I intend to challenge the argument that the WADA believes is their strongest argument for their prohibited list. Namely, that doping is contrary to the *spirit of sport*. However, this argument raises some central questions. What is the spirit of sport? Who decides what the spirit of sport is? Should we always punish an action because it is contrary to the spirit of sport? I want to show that the argument about the spirit of sport is extremely vague and that use of doping, given WADA's vague definition, is not always contrary to the spirit of sport. Moreover, even the most common acts of sport such as playing cowardly in football (where the player quickly passes the ball to avoid making a mistake) or lack of joy on the field will be contrary to the spirit of sport. So why are these actions not banned according to WADA? They should be if we entertain the idea that an action is immoral and should be punishable if it is contrary to the spirit of sport. This is another example of the double standards of the anti-doping proponents.

In Chapter 3, I consider the fact that athletes serve as role models for young people. The fact that athletes are role models have made some politicians and sports managers fear that if doping is allowed and athletes use doping, it might inspire young athletes or fans to use doping as well. And that is not a viable path for young people since doping is harmful. However, this argument is problematic for several reasons. The argument assumes the very thing that must be proven: Namely, that doping is immoral because it is harmful. However, as I will clarify in Chapter 1, doping, within some boundaries, is not harmful, quite the contrary. So if young people become inspired by older and more seasoned athletes to use doping, this would be unproblematic from a moral standpoint. The argument has other flaws. Is it a fair requirement that simply because athletes are considered as role models, they should not use doping? What if you are not a role model, should you then be allowed to use doping? And is there any correlation at all between what the so-called role models do and what young people, who look up to those role models, do? Under any circumstance, we can see that most young fans are hardly as disciplined as the elite athletes and therefore do not imitate their idols in everything they do. And if a correlation should exist in some areas between athletes and their young fans, it is unclear whether the young people will necessarily imitate their role models in a certain area – such as using doping.

Chapter 4 clarifies and criticises the following argument: If doping is allowed, you might fear that athletes who do not want to use doping will experience a morally problematic pressure to use doping. And since athletes should not be exposed to such pressure, we should not allow doping. But how exactly should we understand 'a morally problematic pressure'? And is it always morally unacceptable, all things considered, that athletes are exposed to such pressure? In this chapter, I will argue, inter alia, that elite sport is characterised by athletes being exposed to a significant pressure, but also that this pressure is typically morally unproblematic. The same should apply to the pressure that athletes would experience if doping became allowed. However, as I clearly state in Chapter 4, it is naturally only morally acceptable for athletes to use doping if they are not *directly coerced* (or forced) against their will to use doping. So, from a moral perspective, the difference between direct coercion and what is sometimes called social pressure is very important.

The focus of Chapter 5 is the argument that allowing doping would lead to an inefficient 'arms race' that the athletes would oppose. The idea is that everyone who wants to be a part of sport and who also wants to win must use doping. Yet, the consequences of this arms race are that no one will gain a competitive edge, while the athletes must pay the health-related and financial costs of using doping. I want to show that this type of argumentation rests on some problematic assumptions. For instance, as illustrated in Chapter 1, it is far from certain that use of doping is harmful. Whether that is the case depends on the type of doping in question and how it is administered. Furthermore, it is not obvious that athletes actually want a doping-free sport. The fact that several athletes actually use doping even though it is banned or illegal shows that they want to use doping.

In Chapter 6, I present and criticise the argument that use of doping and possible legalisation of doping will create unfair or uneven competition among the athletes. Using doping in competitive sports is naturally cheating and thus unfair, because it is a breach of adopted rules that you silently accept when you participate in sports competitions. However, the current doping rules are not carved in stone, and if doping was legal, it would not be cheating. In this chapter, I also clarify that an ultimate requirement for fair competition in the world of sports is problematic for several reasons. I wish to argue that sport is essentially unfair. The reason being that it is unfair that people who have won in the genetic and social lottery are either much better at elite sports or have better financial conditions for participating in elite sports than those less fortunate. This inequality is unfair because it is a result of factors over which the athlete has no control. The ideal of fair competition proposes the sympathetic idea that we should strive for all athletes having the same opportunities of performing at a high level. But, doping does not have to be contrary to this ideal. I want to show that a legalisation of doping will be able to challenge this conventional way of thinking and actually increase competitive equality among athletes.

Chapter 7 is a run-off heat where I intend to present and critically discuss four anti-doping arguments that are not prominent in the doping debate. However, since I want to give the anti-doping proponents the best hand, I will not consciously omit discussions of a number of further arguments that conclude that doping is immoral. The four arguments emphasise that doping is immoral either because doping is unnatural or because doping is detrimental to a central and attractive element of the sport (the fact that the outcome is not given). Or because doping promotes a game other than sport or because doping makes it difficult to identify with the doped athlete. In this chapter, I will show that doping is not unnatural; that doping is not detrimental to one of the key attractions of sport; that doping does not promote a game other than sport and that doping does in fact not mean that the spectators cannot identify with doped athletes.

The following presents a short summary of the arguments at play in the quest to convince us that the current doping policy is morally justifiable:

Doping should be prohibited because doping is unhealthy

Doping should be prohibited because doping is contrary to the spirit of sport

Doping should be prohibited because doping inspires children/young people to use doping

Doping should be prohibited because allowing it would pressure athletes into using doping

Doping should be prohibited because athletes do not want to dope

Doping should be prohibited because doping leads to unfair competition

Doping should be prohibited because doping is unnatural

Doping should be prohibited because doping is detrimental to the attraction of sport

Doping should be prohibited because doping promotes a game other than sport

Doping should be prohibited because doping makes it impossible to identify with the athlete.

Let the game begin!

Notes

1 For the problem, that WADA's rules are far from being harmonised throughout the world and therefore create issues of unfairness, see, e.g. Dimeo and Møller (2018, pp. 67–75).
2 For a discussion of the last point, see Petersen and Frias (2020).
3 Pound (2006).
4 WADA (2020). https://www.wada-ama.org/en/content/what-is-prohibited (accessed June 3, 2020).
5 Hartgens and Kuipers (2004).
6 Johnson (2016).
7 Savulescu, Foddy, and Clayton (2004, p. 666).
8 Ulrich, Pope, and Cléret (2018).
9 Pitsch and Emrich (2012).
10 See, e.g. Dimeo and Møller (2018, pp. 63–66).
11 Savulescu and Foddy (2011).
12 Rasmussen and Wivel (2013).
13 The haematocrit level describes the percentage of red blood cells relative to the total blood volume.
14 Hood (2017).
15 Møller (2010, p. 71).
16 See, e.g. Ibid., pp. 4–12 or Mazanov (2016, pp. 18–28).

17 WADA (2020).
18 Until WADA formulated its prohibited list, a number of sports federations and associations had since the 1960s had their own lists.
19 WADA (2020).
20 Tamburrini (2000). For criticism of Tamburrini, see, e.g. Petersen and Kristensen (2009).
21 In contexts other than this book, I have argued in favour of this viewpoint; see, e.g. Petersen and Lippert-Rasmussen (2007). Savulescu et al. (2004) have reached the same conclusion, only through somewhat different arguments.
22 To my knowledge, no athlete has been tested positive for gene doping.
23 For an excellent discussion of gene doping, see Tamburrini and Tännsjö (2005).
24 See, e.g. Hass and Healey (2016).
25 Under Danish legislation, an athlete will not be punished if a test reveals use of any of these drugs or methods – see Act No. 232 of 21 April 1999 on prohibition against certain doping use (retsinfo.dk).
26 UK Department for Digital, Culture, Media & Sport (2017). The states of, e.g. Italy, France, Spain and the USA have criminalised the use of doping, see, e.g. Kayser (2009, p. 162).
27 Chomiak, Junge, Peterson & Dvorak (2016).
28 Coyle (2005).
29 Møller (2010, p. 9).

1 Doping and health

Everyone can agree that the athletes' health should play a central role when we discuss and determine what substances and methods should feature on an anti-doping list. Few sensible persons would want the Olympic Games, Wimbledon or Tour de France to lead to fatalities among athletes. The most common and obvious argument against doping starts with this very assumption, that doping is harmful and might at worst be fatal.[1]

However, it is worth mentioning that before the anti-doping policy emerged at the beginning of the 1960s, not a single fatality had been recorded in the world of sports that is known for sure to relate to the use of doping.[2] That means that for a period of approx. 3,000 years, from ancient Greece and until the 1960s, when doping was not prohibited, and when it was common to use various performance-enhancing drugs, no one is able to confirm with certainty that anyone has died because of doping. Add in the fact that many sports were more dangerous and challenging than they are today – for instance a six-day cycling race, actually consisted of six full days of racing and boxing matches were only settled once one of the boxers was knocked out. Prominent historians and sports scientists have also documented that doping was widespread before 1965.[3]

Unfortunately, it is also true that doping in some cases has resulted in fatalities. Studies indicate that the use of EPO at the end of the 1980s was probably the cause of death among young Dutch and Belgian riders, whose blood became too thick causing them to die from blood clots.[4] However, it should also be mentioned that in the past approximately 30 years of cycling there has been no record of deaths that can directly be ascribed to doping. This is remarkable since research indicate that doping has been widely used in cycling during most of this period.[5] Besides possible deaths following abuse of doping, doping may also have other adverse effects. For instance, abuse and wrong use of anabolic steroids may cause cardiovascular diseases, severe liver damage, reduced fertility and lack of impulse control.[6] However, there are three aspects that we need to clarify if we believe that doping should be illegal because it is harmful for the athletes.

First, use of doping substances and methods that feature on the prohibited list does not necessarily have an adverse effect on health. On the contrary, it may in some situations, as illustrated in the following, boost health to use doping. Second, there might be some advantages of legalising doping, even if the use of doping, in isolation, can be harmful. Third, it seems like a double standard wanting to prohibit a substance that might be harmful in some situations, while also believing that we should not prohibit sports like American football, boxing, cycling, motor sports and show jumping. These sports are all examples of sports that to a large degree not only *can* be but also often *are* harmful and claim several lives each year. If we, from a moral perspective, accept that athletes should be allowed to participate in sports that can be harmful, we should also accept that athletes are allowed to use doping even if doping can be harmful. Let's take a closer look at each of these three aspects.

Use of doping can be healthy

There is no doubt that it is unhealthy and dangerous to participate in a professional boxing event or a race like the Tour de France. After a tough stage in the Tour, the riders' bodies are drained of, e.g. red blood cells and testosterone. In these situations, it may promote health if the riders are given red blood cells artificially (e.g. via EPO) and testosterone instead of letting them continue with a broken down body.[7] Just read what doctor Andreas Hartkopp has been quoted as saying in a newspaper:

> Both testosterone levels and the number of red blood cells drop during considerable physical strain. For a rider it would make really good sense to supplement what he is lacking. Just like taking a vitamin pill to supplement what you cannot get through your diet. It would also make sense to supplement with a bit of EPO to increase the haemoglobin percentage.[8]

Alternatively, the use of intravenous drip may help 'speed up' the absorption of water, salts, minerals and sugar. This allows the athlete after a tough competition to recover quicker and less painfully than if he/she took salt and sugar orally. The quicker the body recovers, the quicker our immune system is reset and the less vulnerable we will be to infections and other diseases. Accordingly, the use of certain substances and methods on WADA's prohibited list may in some cases improve the athletes' health.[9]

Further, several studies show that even though doping may not benefit athletes it, e.g. EPO, can be safe to use:

> The metabolic and hormonal and renal effects of EPO do not seem to range beyond acceptable limits and are reversible. Taken together, EPO seems safe to use for experimental purposes in healthy volunteers[10]

When doping might even promote health or can be safe to use, why then be so afraid of the drugs and punish people who use doping? The doping debate shows an obvious mismatch between the clear moral rejection of letting athletes use doping because it is believed to be harmful and the lack of reference to data that clearly shows that doping, even in *limited and physician-controlled amounts*, is harmful. In an attempt to demonstrate the danger of a drug like EPO, you cannot just point to the allegedly many young riders who died due to excessive use of EPO at the end of the 1980s. Because since then – at least to my knowledge – no one has been able to document that athletes have died due to excessive use of EPO. This positive development is probably due to the fact that sports physicians and athletes now know more about EPO than they did when EPO was a new drug on the market. If EPO had been allowed 30 years ago, the abuse of EPO would probably not have taken place in hiding, administered by eccentric physicians or self-medicating fanatics, and the young riders would probably still be alive. Paradoxically, there is reason to say that the doping prohibition tempts athletes to use new drugs because tests have not been developed to reveal their use.[11] However, the use of new drugs increases the risk that the athletes are harmed, as there is often less knowledge about the new doping drugs compared to the well-known drugs. So the current ban on doping may possibly cause more deaths than a regulated form of free doping.

Some athletes even believe that doping use may increase the safety in sports. American skier Bode Miller has said:

> I'm surprised it's [EPO and other drugs] illegal. Because in our sport, it would be pretty minimal health risks, and it would actually make it safer for the athletes, because you'd have less chance of making a mistake at the bottom and killing yourself.[12]

I do not know whether Miller is right in this assumption. But under any circumstance, it would be ill advised to simply assume that all use of doping would be harmful. And even in situations where doping – in isolation – can be harmful for the individual athlete there are two further aspects that we need to settle before we with certainty can assert that WADA's doping policy is the best way of ensuring the athletes' health. First, we must demand that a doping prohibition is held up against the advantages it might have to legalise doping under regulated terms. Second, we need to answer the moral question that addresses where the lines should be drawn in terms of the extent to which an athlete should be allowed to expose him/herself to actions that might be harmful to his/her health. In the following, I will approach these two aspects in succession.

Advantages of releasing doping

Today we see how some types of doping are manufactured in shady facilities without adequate control of product quality. Add in the fact that doping is distributed in a black and criminal market. A black market is often unregulated in terms of price and quality. We therefore have every reason to believe that the control of the quality, shelf life, quantity and use of the doping is poorer than it would be in a white and regulated market. This means that the first advantage of legalising substances like EPO and anabolic steroids would be that use of doping in a market regulated by doctors and health authorities would probably make it safer for the doping users compared to the current black market.[13] So by relaxing the anti-doping rules, the athletes will be given better access to healthy use of doping. The athletes will be able to keep in regular contact with physicians who can tell them about side effects and the proper dosage and quality, so that the risk to their health is as little as possible.

A second advantage of legalising doping is that you reduce the possibility of *criminals profiting* from producing, distributing, stealing and selling doping. As, e.g. Alessandro Donati and others have shown in several studies, international organised crime make millions of euros on a black market for substances such as anabolic steroids and EPO.[14] A third advantage is that legalisation will minimise the possibilities of some *athletes coming into contact with criminal environments.* A contact that may lead to bad networks and more crime. Fourth, legalisation will typically mean that fewer are punished, which has the immediate advantage that you, all else being equal, can *save money* on testing athletes, investigation and court cases. Finally, legalisation will mean that athletes (and their family and friends) avoid the *welfare loss* often associated with being punished for doping. This may be a welfare loss associated with the public humiliation and stigmatisation that typically accompanies being punished for using doping. Or it may be the costs – for particularly professional athletes – associated with loss of future earnings and seizing of earlier prize money. Athletes can also lose the identity many of them have in relation to their sport and their social relations if they are punished for using doping. The racing cyclist Michael Rasmussen has for instance accused the anti-doping rules of causing several riders to suffer from depression and possibly commit suicide following a doping conviction.[15]

All these problematic issues – use of potentially harmful drugs; earning potential for criminal environments; athletes' contact with criminal environments and stigmatisation and conviction of athletes – would be diminished if we legalised doping under regulated terms. I have to my surprise noted that the political debate on whether cannabis should be legalised considers all the above issues. However, in the doping debate the advantages of legalising are completely absent.

Doping can be harmful – but the same applies to sport

Prohibiting doping because it may be harmful is a viewpoint that does not correlate with accepting sport that may constitute a health risk.

For instance, intense physical exercise increases the chance of stress injuries and weakens the immune system. Moreover, some sports involve a direct danger to the athletes' lives. American football, boxing, mountain climbing, cycling, ice hockey, skiing, horse riding and motor sports all claim several lives each year. In the USA alone, approx. 300 people have, in the period from 1970 till today, died following injuries they have sustained by playing American football.[16] Injuries that have typically occurred when the players at great speed ram their heads together either in an attempt to stop each other's path or when they try to get a hold of the oval ball. During the same period, thousands of American football players have suffered severe mental problems due to repeated concussions, which also put them at higher risk of developing, e.g. depression and sclerosis.[17] But these risks do not keep people from choosing these types of sport. And many will still think that it is not immoral to participate in and allow sports that cost lives each year. However it does seem like a double standard if you believe that doping is morally wrong because it is harmful, while still thinking that sports that are harmful are not.

If we accept that athletes are allowed to participate in sports that are harmful to their health, we should also accept that an athlete uses doping even if it might also be harmful. Naturally, under the condition that we try to reduce the harmful acts that may arise out of doping by introducing safety values and providing medical information about effects and side effects. This goes along with the way sport is regulated today. One example of a measure to reduce the number of injuries in sports is the mandatory use of helmets in cycling. But note that most sports associations do not believe that we should reduce the risk of injury to zero since there are other values at stake in sports. Values that sometimes are allowed to trump the regard for athlete health. Values such as suspense, entertainment, tradition and intensity in, e.g. competitive sports where we compromise with the safety and health of the athletes.

If the athletes' health was our only moral concern, we would have to render sports unrecognisable. We would have to prevent Formula 1 racers from driving faster than 50 km/h. If we do not want to allow that sport is harmful, we would probably only be able to allow certain board games like chess, backgammon and checkers. However, it should then only be allowed to play and spend time on these board games for a defined period of time, since hour-long board games combined with the players' preoccupation and fascination might affect their mental health negatively. Hour-long board games can also be a harmful time thief that can lead to lack of sleep making you unable to do your job or take care of your family. Moreover, a board game should only be allowed if it could be played in a rubber cell so that you would not get injured or hurt if you slipped from your chair due to fatigue or if you fell from your chair while celebrating wildly after yelling "checkmate!".

So I allow myself to assume that few would believe that sports that might be harmful should also be punishable. Or put in more general terms: If we accept that we should punish harmful acts, this would have the unreasonable consequence that we would also have to accept that driving a car, drinking alcohol, constructing metros and bridges, doing surgery or using ice picks by definition should be criminal acts, as these actions too have caused harm (and are likely to continue to cause harm) to people.

In literature on sports ethics, many attempts have been made to escape this double standard view where you morally accept that sports can be harmful, but still believe that doping is morally wrong because it is harmful. One suggestion to get out of this double standard is to establish a distinction between injuries that are *internal* in relation to the sport and injuries that are *external* in relation to the sport. The injuries that are linked to doping can be considered as external in relation to the sport. For instance, a professional racing cyclist can avoid any harmful effects of using, e.g. EPO – thickened blood with the accompanying risk of blood clots – by not using EPO. However, the athlete will still be a racing cyclist. According to this line of thought, external injuries like doping should be prohibited. However, the risk of crashing during a descent or being hit by a car in training are examples of internal injuries related to competitive cycling. Contrary to doping, being hit by a car or crashing during a race is an example of risks of injuries that a racing cyclist cannot avoid without having to stop being a racing cyclist. They are injuries or risks of injuries that comes with being a racing cyclist and which should therefore not be punishable.

However, there are at least two problems if you believe that this distinction may warrant a moral distinction between injuries caused by sport and injuries caused by doping. First, if athletes are allowed to become injured while doing their sport as long as it does not relate to external matters, we end up in the unreasonable situation that a racing cyclist or a football player should not be allowed to do weight training or cardio by running. The reason is that the injuries that might arise out of these activities are external in relation to the sport. Indeed, you can be a racing cyclist or football player even if you do not lift weights or cardio.

Second, it seems arbitrary to make a moral distinction between internal and external injury and accept that an internal injury is less ethically problematic than an external injury. The injuries linked with the actual sport, such as riding extremely fast down a mountain in the Tour de France can vary a lot. A rider may go for broke and risk his/her life by riding extremely aggressively down a mountain in pouring rain and then gain an advantage against the other riders who have chosen to ride more cautiously. However, is it more morally right for the rider to expose himself and his family and friends to this dangerous descent than if he uses blood doping administered and monitored by physicians and also chooses to ride cautiously down a mountain in the Tour? According to the internal/external injury distinction, the first scenario is preferable to the latter as the latter scenario only entails a risk of external injury.

However, if your son was the rider, what risk would you prefer? If your son rode like a mad man down a mountain in pouring rain instead of a controlled descent with some of the natural hormone EPO in his blood? Personally, I have no doubt and would prefer that my son rode sensibly and took physician-controlled EPO instead of riding down the mountain with contempt for death.[18]

Another attempt at arguing for why we should accept harmful sports but not harmful doping is that the latter should be considered as an additional risk added to an already harmful sport. So by forbidding doping, you reduce the sum of health injuries the athletes are exposed to. However, this line of thought suffers from two faults. First, the argument assumes that a doping ban will reduce the number of injuries athletes are exposed to. But as I have described earlier in this chapter, this is far from certain, since there are a number of advantages (also in terms of health) of legalising doping. Second, the world of sports regularly accepts new measures that increase the number of injuries. Accepting new sports like snowboarding or base jumping, accepting new elements in ice skating or in skate and kite boarding and accepting that more people join traditional and harmful sports all increase the number of harmful acts in sports. But if you accept the increase in harmful acts, then why not also accept measures like doping even if it increases the number of harmful acts in the world of sports?

My viewpoint that, e.g. EPO should not be on the prohibited list is naturally a controversial one. Controversial because it is well known that if the number of red blood cells exceeds 50%, the blood will become too thick, which may cause blood clots and other complications. However, if use of EPO can be harmful, why then does WADA allow a practice where you increase the number of red blood cells by means of altitude training, oxygen equipment, oxygen tents and so-called altitude houses (houses with a low oxygen percentage)? Again, the current doping policy appears like a double standard. At least two rationales are presented in the attempt to justify a distinction between use of EPO and other legal methods for increasing the number of red blood cells.

You could say that injecting EPO into your body is *unnatural* and therefore immoral. But why then is it not unnatural and immoral to use altitude houses, oxygen tents or oxygen equipment to achieve the same effect as you get from EPO? In Chapter 7, I will show in detail why the unnatural claim in the doping debate is problematic.

Another rationale for prohibiting EPO but still accepting use of altitude houses and altitude training is that EPO may be more dangerous to use and easier to abuse. As far as I know, there are limits to how high the haematocrit level can become by means of altitude training, while that is not the case when injecting EPO. It can therefore be easier to abuse or use too much EPO. So since EPO is more dangerous to use than, e.g. altitude training and oxygen tents, we have *one* good reason for prohibiting EPO while accepting altitude training and oxygen tents. Yet, this line of thought is not without flaws. Because simply because you abuse a substance, it does not naturally imply that the substance should be prohibited. Drinking water can also lead to abuse. If you drink large amounts of water, you deplete your body of vital salts and minerals and increase the risk of serious injury and death. We need to make sure that we do not exclusively focus on a possible abuse but also look at the actual improvements that will follow a legalisation of doping such as EPO.

If EPO is legalised, it will naturally be good to follow-up with tests of the athletes.[19] If the anti-doping organisations want to focus on the athletes' health, they should focus on the values that show the number of red blood cells in the body (e.g. by measuring the haematocrit level). This is a strategy that has to be used by the International Cycling Union (UCI). If a rider had his haematocrit level measured at over 50% of the blood volume immediately before a competition, the rider will not be allowed to compete for two weeks.[20]

So if we want healthier athletes, we should legalise most of the substances and methods on WADA's prohibited list. Instead of a long prohibited list, we should test for safety values and not test for the cause of the elevated values. So my proposal is – using EPO as an example: Do not test whether an athlete has used a pharmaceutical product like EPO, but whether her haematocrit level is over 50%. The reason for the athlete having a level over 50% – whether due to altitude training, oxygen tents, altitude houses, drugs – is of no consequence. What is important is that the value does not exceed what is deemed safe.

Still there are other arguments against free doping that have nothing to do with athlete health. In the following, I will focus on the World Anti-Doping Agency (WADA), which believes that the key argument for punishing use of doping is that it is contrary to *the spirit of sport*.

Notes

1 See, e.g. WADA (2019).
2 Møller (2010, p. 33, 36).
3 Møller (2010, p. 42).
4 Eichner (2007); see also Kious (2008). However, doubts have been raised as to whether the riders mentioned actually died because of EPO – see, e.g. López (2011).
5 Møller (2010, p. 43).
6 See, e.g. WADA leaflet (2020).
7 See, e.g. Savulescu and Foddy (2011).
8 *Weekendavisen* (Danish newspaper), July 1, 2005.
9 For examples of how EPO can promote health in ways other than those mentioned in the above-mentioned, see, e.g. Bailey, Robach, Thomsen, and Lundby (2006) and Ninot, Connes, and Caillaud (2006).

10 Lundby and Olsen (2011, p. 1265). See also Johnson (2016, p. 195): "Under a hematologist's expert care, EPO is safe. The drug saves thousands of lives every year".

11 Møller (2010, pp. 42–43).

12 Rugh (2005). Legalize it. https://www.skiracing.com/stories/bode-millers-take-doping-alpine-skiing-legalize-it.

13 For several of these observation see also Kayser (2009) and Johnson (2016, p. 299).

14 See, e.g. Donati (2007) and Paoli and Donati (2013) and Hunt (2011).

15 Rasmussen and Wivel (2013). For examples of these observations on suicide and depression because of being punished for testing positive for the use of doping, see also Dimeo and Møller (2018, pp. 118–124).

16 Mueller and Colgate (2013, pp. 19–20).

17 See, e.g. Pryor, Larson, and DeBeliso (2016) and Abel (2007).

18 See also Kious (2008) for a critique of this use of the internal/external distinction.

19 Increased testing of haematocrit level will naturally entail additional costs, yet if you do not test for EPO, you can save money since a recombinant EPO test is much more expensive than a haematocrit test. See, e.g. Abbott (2000).

20 Møller (2010, p. 9).

2 Doping and the spirit of sport

WADA's central argument against doping is that doping must be prohibited because it is contrary to the spirit of sport. But before I engage in a critical discussion of this argument, it would be appropriate to provide a short description of the history of WADA and what characterises the organisation.

WADA was established in 1999 on the initiative of the International Olympic Committee (IOC) as a direct response to the doping scandal in the Tour de France in 1998. WADA is supported by most national and international sports associations and by governments, national organisations (like Anti Doping Danmark) and transnational organisations like the EU. The foundation board of WADA consists of 38 persons and is composed equally of representatives from the Olympic Movement and governments. The first head of WADA was Dick Pound who held office from 1999 to 2007. The present president is Wilton Banka. WADA's official goal is to ensure athlete health, promote the fight against doping so that we get a doping-free sport and to harmonise nations in respect of which substances and methods should be prohibited and how and when athletes should be tested. Finally, WADA decides the punishment of doping users and the maximum penalty for athletes violating WADA's prohibited list.

When WADA selects the substances or methods that should feature on the prohibited list, it does so by applying the following rule: If, and only if, *two out of three* of the following conditions are met, should a substance or a method be included on the prohibited list:

- If the substance or method actually has a *performance-enhancing effect* or has the potential to enhance performance
- If the use of the substance or method actually constitutes a *health risk* or has the potential of constituting a health risk

- If the use of the substance of method is contrary to the *spirit of sport* as described in the WADA code.[1]

This 2-out-of-3 rule appears sensible at first glance. Sensible as it would have unreasonable consequences if only one condition or if all three conditions would have to be met in order for a substance or method to be featured on the prohibited list. If only one of the conditions needs to be met, it would have the unreasonable consequence that, e.g. bread and water would have to be included on the prohibited list. Because, bread and water has a performance-enhancing effect. Yet, an army marches on its stomach as the old phrase goes. But despite the fact that WADA has a comprehensive prohibited list, it would naturally be morally unreasonable and impossible to enforce rules that mean that you have to forbid athletes from drinking water and eating bread.

The rationale for only two and not all three conditions having to be met is that if all conditions need to be met, it would be impossible to prohibit, e.g. gene doping in case it turns out not to constitute a health risk to the athlete. Gene doping is a type of doping based on gene therapy. Gene therapy involves altering or modifying a patient's cells for the purpose of fighting disease. Gene therapy used to fight serious diseases like cancer is, at the time of writing, not recognised as treatment but is still being studied in trials. However, expectations are very high. Gene doping, however, is non-therapeutic and seeks instead to alter or modify the athlete's cells for the purpose of enhancing the athlete's performance.[2] As far as I know, no athletes have been convicted of using gene doping. But there can be little doubt that if or when gene therapy becomes readily available, it will engender a massive potential for athletes wanting to dope or enhance their performance.

A substance or a method that is performance enhancing in relation to a sports performance or that constitutes a health risk is relatively easy to understand linguistically. However, when you use the spirit of sport as an argument, it raises at least three issues that I intend to answer in succession and which overall constitute WADA's Achilles' heel: What is the spirit of sport? Why is it immoral to act contrary to the spirit of sport? When is use of doping contrary to the spirit of sport? In terms of the first question, WADA tries to add some substance to the notion of the spirit of sport by offering the following characterisation: Spirit of sport characterises "... the essence of Olympism and the celebration of the human spirit"[3] and consists of the following 11 values:

Ethics, fair play and honesty
Health

Excellence in performance
Character and education
Fun and joy
Teamwork
Dedication and commitment
Respect for rules and laws
Respect for self and other participants
Courage
Community and solidarity

One obvious interpretation of this list is that it should not purport to describe what characterises sport. Instead, it should show the ideal for sport, or as WADA intends, what should be the ideal for sport. The list includes various values and traits that everyone would probably find appealing. Most people would probably approve if sport is healthy and involves fun and joy, teamwork, courage and community. And as Mike McNamee has argued, this can be understood as a strength of WADA's code.[4]

But when WADA wants to use the spirit of sport in its rationale for which substances and methods should be included on the prohibited list, they run into a host of challenges.[5] First, WADA allows the spirit of sport to play two different but incompatible roles in its rationale for what substances and methods should be prohibited for athletes to use. As just described, the spirit of sport is presented as one condition out of three equally important conditions. But at the same time, WADA makes it clear that the spirit of sport is the foundation of their entire anti-doping policy. WADA writes that "Doping is fundamentally contrary to the spirit of sport".[6]

To clarify why these two roles are incompatible, we need to envisage the following situation: We have a substance or a method X, that (i) does not enhance performance and (ii) does not constitute a risk to the athletes' health but (iii) is contrary to the spirit of sport. X might be the use of intravenous drip to give the athlete a sugar and saline solution to ensure that the athlete recuperates quickly after a tough competition. Use of intravenous drip is a method – regardless of what such a drip contains (even water) – that features on WADA's prohibited list. However, if the fundamental rationale for WADA's fight against doping is to protect the spirit of sport, while the spirit of sport forms part of a 2-out-of-3 rule, WADA's reference to the spirit of sport becomes contradictory. Because if the spirit of sport is a fundamental principle and use of intravenous drip is contrary to the spirit of sport, then it should be punishable. But according to the 2-out-of-3 rule, the use of intravenous drip should not be punishable since it does not immediately enhance the sports performance or cause a risk to the athletes' health. So when WADA uses the spirit of sport as rationale for what to include on the prohibited list, you can easily get confused over what role exactly WADA wants the spirit of sport to play.[7]

Second: What will WADA do or think if a sports activity *conflicts* with some of the values that according to WADA characterise the spirit of sport? Will WADA, for instance, find that participating in the Tour de France is contrary to the spirit of sport? On the one hand, it appears obvious that participation in the race is an expression of 'courage' and 'dedication', but on the other hand, participation in the Tour hardly meets the value of 'fun and joy' or 'health'. But what then should we think when a race cyclist participates in the Tour de France? Is it contrary to the spirit of sport? If the answer is yes, then WADA should strive to prohibit the Tour de France. But since it is clear that WADA is not intending to prohibit the Tour de France, it is natural to interpret its answer as a resounding No. So if participation in the Tour de France is not contrary to the spirit of sport, even though participation in this tough race does not honour all the values listed in WADA's description of the spirit of sport, then it appears as a double standard that WADA at the same time prohibits an athlete from doping. For using doping appears exactly to be consistent with values like teamwork, courage, dedication and commitment and excellence in performance, although doping is probably contrary to the value fun and joy. And what position would WADA take on a football player who respects the laws and rules and eats healthy year round, but plays a cowardly game of football – is he acting contrary to the spirit of sport? He exhibits anything but courage on the field. If the cowardly football player acts contrary to the spirit of sport, then he should be punished in the same way as the athletes who use doping.

However, if the cowardly football player should be punished, WADA would be extremely busy punishing myriad of athletes who fail to show courage on the field, on the horse, in the car or wherever they do their sport. So if WADA believes that the football player is not acting contrary to the spirit of sport – even though it is obvious that he is acting contrary to some of the values contained in WADA's understanding of the spirit of sport – what then is WADA's rationale for this position? The problem is that in such situations, WADA unfortunately has no clear strategy for how to weigh the values of the spirit of sport against each other. The fact that WADA fails to make it clear how to apply the spirit of sport to identify immoral and punishable acts is a massive problem, or in other words, an Achilles' heel. It is an Achilles' heel for WADA because the spirit of sport is presented as the fundamental principle behind WADA's rationale for what substances and methods should be prohibited. It is, unfortunately, a principle that is extremely vague and difficult to apply.

Third: How does WADA *know* that a substance or method is contrary to the spirit of sport? Riding the Tour de France with an auxiliary engine on your bike seems for obvious reasons to be contrary to the spirit of sport. This would allow an unfit, old person, who might not even be able to ride a bike on his own, to win the Tour. "Running" a marathon with a propeller on the back falls into the same category. But is it contrary to the spirit of sport to use an electric car to transport golf players from one tee to the next? What about the use of caffeine? Caffeine used to be on the doping list, but has now been removed. What is the rationale behind intense coffee drinking not being contrary to the spirit of sport according to WADA (but being on the prohibited list before 2004) and therefore not prohibited? Is it really so, that an action is contrary to the spirit of sport simply because some people on the foundation board of WADA by a show of hands and without proper justification have decided that is how it should be? That actually seems to be the case. If this is true, then the Home Mission's rationale against dancing (that dancing between two adults of opposite sex leads to promiscuity) stands as clear mathematical proof compared to WADA's use of the spirit of sport.

On the one hand, WADA believes that it is consistent with the spirit of sport to train in a high-pressure chamber, use disc wheels, drink cola, coffee or energy drinks with a high caffeine content or take creatine, which can increase muscle power. All methods or substances capable of enhancing the athlete's performance and that are usually not harmful. Yet, on the other hand, WADA believes that it is contrary to the spirit of sport to use methods (like intravenous drip) that to the same extent are capable of enhancing the athlete's performance, but when used under competent medical guidance are hardly harmful. So why is it that only the latter method is contrary to the spirit of sport and not the use of the other substances?

Fourth: How can we be certain that WADA has provided *the right description* of the spirit of sport? Why not take the position that doping is consistent with the spirit of sport? Excellence in performance is central to most sports, and pharmaceutical products may help athletes perform excellently.

I have tried to show that the principle that an action must be consistent with the spirit of sport as defined by WADA raises a number of issues. First, it is unclear what status this principle has in WADA's rationale for what substances and methods should be featured on the prohibited list. It seems contradictory and in any event highly problematic that WADA allows the principle of the spirit of sport to serve as both a fundamental rationale for its entire perspective on doping policy and as one out of three equal principles. Second, even if we assume that the spirit of sport simply plays a fundamental role in the rationale behind its doping policy, there are obvious problems in applying a principle that contains 11 very different values. In respect of both using certain substances and practising a sport (e.g. by doing a sport in a cowardly manner), a conflict might occur between the values that WADA believes constitute the spirit of sport. However, it is unclear how WADA intends to handle such conflicts. And even though these problems are solved, it is far from evident that WADA's definition of the spirit of sport is the right one.

Despite this criticism, I believe that WADA's work to inform of the possible health risks of using doping and to test athletes for violating the health-related safety values is morally necessary and important. However, I suggest that WADA and other anti-doping organisations focus on athlete health and leave vague ramblings about the spirit of sport to the private sphere or occult organisations.

Notes

1 WADA (2019, p. 30). Let's disregard that WADA also includes substances or methods that do not meet any of these conditions but which have the potential to blur prohibited substances or methods on the prohibited list.
2 WADA (2020, p. 7).
3 WADA (2019, p. 14).
4 McNamee (2012).
5 There are many scholars who have expressed the scepticism towards the applicability of these 11 values in justifying which substances and methods should be on WADA's prohibited list. See, e.g. McNamee (2012).
6 Ibid.
7 For this type of objection, see Petersen and Lippert-Rasmussen (2007). For a similar criticism of WADA's use of the spirit of sport as rationale for what substances and methods that should be included on the prohibited list, see Savulescu, Foddy, and Clayton (2004) and Møller (2010, pp. 13–14).

3　Doping and role models

There is little doubt that top athletes like Cristiano Ronaldo and Serena Williams act as inspiring role models for many children and young people. However the existence of role models also serves as a premise in an argument against doping. A premise that emphasises that we can protect children and young people against doping by prohibiting doping among adult athletes. Former Vice President of WADA, Brian Mikkelsen, has put forward a similar argument:

> But the doping issue is not just about elite sports. Fighting doping is also about ensuring that our children and young people have some heroes to look up to – not medicated machines, not wonders created in the lab – but doping-free athletes of flesh and blood. Today, sport is such a vital element of young people's lives and self-perception... that we need to make sure that fair play and healthy competition wins.[1]

Mikkelsen is far from the only one to reject the use of doping by referring to the negative impact doped role models can have on children and young people. When the swimmer Michael Phelps was posted on front pages worldwide in 2009 in a picture that showed him hitting the bong, the Olympic Committee made the following statement:

> Michael is a role model, and he is well aware of the responsibilities and accountability that come with setting a positive example for others, particularly young people. In this instance, regrettably, he failed to fulfill those responsibilities.[2]

But before engaging in a more critical discussion of this manner of arguing, we should be aware that the argument can be presented in at least two different ways: One where the use of doping among top athletes, besides 'inspiring' children and young people to have a go at doping, will inspire young people to use euphoriants like cannabis and cocaine[3]; and another where the concern primarily is that young fans will become inspired to use doping without starting using euphoriants. In the following, I will only focus on the latter. I make this choice because I believe that we should be careful to compare euphoriants with the use of doping in sports, since athletes are often very preoccupied by bodily health. Use of euphoriants like cannabis, cocaine and morphine are typically contradictory to being able to perform at your best as an athlete. All athletes know this, as do probably most children and young people who engage in sport and have athletes as their role models.[4]

So, a central concern is that if doping is legalised and used by role models, then children and young people would become inspired to use doping which would be harmful to them.[5] As most others, I'm generally very positive to this line of thought. If doping is legalised and adult role models inspire children and young people to hurt themselves via doping, we should naturally worry and try to prevent them from being hurt. That being said, I believe that the role model argument should be given the red card. Allow me to focus on three challenges facing this line of thought and then finish with a small personal anecdote about my children and the use of doping.

The role model argument is given the red card

First, it would be pure speculation to believe that children under the age of 18 who idolises athletes would try to get their hands on, e.g. EPO or anabolic steroids and use a syringe to inject themselves just because doping becomes legal for adults. Children and young people do not always do the same as their idols. Although many children and young people sometimes imitate the behaviour of an athlete they admire – for instance, get a new hair cut when Cristiano Ronaldo changes his – then they do not imitate everything he does. Indeed, few young people probably get into trouble with the tax authorities just because Ronaldo is. Next time you watch a football match, how many of the spectators idolising the players on the field do you think exercise as much and eat as healthy as those on the field? Probably not that many fans would have that kind of discipline. And how many young boxers have bitten the ear of their opponent simply because Mike Tyson did it in that famous match in 1997? None, as far as I know! So, the first challenge facing the role model argument is that a number of observations oppose the idea that young fans will imitate the athletes.

Add that – to my knowledge – there is no scientific documentation showing that children and young people will use doping because their idols use doping. Children and young people can naturally choose to use doping for completely other reasons than being inspired by their idols. They can choose to use doping because they are concerned with body weight, want to perform better, have poor self-esteem, get picked for elite teams, recover faster or become famous and earn money.[6] This challenge for the role model argument can naturally be solved by presenting research showing that the alleged correlation between athletes who dope and children's and young people's use of doping exists. Only, I have not seen any research results that have been able to prove or render this correlation probable. However, if this research were able to show a correlation, then the argument would still be very weak, as illustrated in the next section.

Another challenge facing the role model argument is much more serious. Because even if you can prove that a correlation exists between role models who use doping and children and young people who use doping, allowing doping, as described in Chapter 1, may in fact result in improved athlete health. Most substances on WADA's prohibited list are not harmful as long as they are used correctly. Being used correctly basically means that the substances are prescribed and monitored by physicians and are only used within certain safety levels. This simple observation is enough to reject the role model argument. If it is true that doping has come to stay and that research shows that a regulated and white market for doping will improve health, then no one would be harmed by allowing doping – on the contrary. It might even be the case that young people aged 18–21 would use doping in a safer manner than today where doping is prohibited. So the role model argument is based on the wrong assumption that doping is immoral because it is harmful.

Even if it would be harmful for children under the age of 18 to use doping, it does not mean that we should also prohibit doping for persons over the age of 18. For instance, it would be quite reasonable to think that some things should be prohibited for children but not for adults. Although it is illegal for children to drink alcohol, smoke tobacco, drive a car and fly a plane, we have not chosen to make these actions illegal for adults. There are some differences between children and adults that make us think that it is morally right for adults and not children to be able to engage in these actions. This might be differences in terms of judgement, responsibility and competency. I fully admit that some children are much wiser than some adults. However, on average there are good reasons to believe that adults are more responsible and more competent to make the right choices regarding their own lives.

Third, it does not seem convincing to let athletes serve as moral spearheads in an educational project for children and young people. At least not more so than other adults trying to make a living. Generally, we would probably not want to punish role models like musicians or parents – who are arguably the most important role models for children – if they choose to live an unhealthy life. Clearly, a singer like Amy Winehouse, who drank alcohol and were sniffing cocaine on stage during her concerts and who sang about not wanting to go into rehab, may inspire a young audience to increase their alcohol consumption. But even though we can take the moral position that adults should be moral role models and that they therefore should not drink or smoke while children and young people are watching, it does not imply that alcohol and tobacco should be illegal to use. So it does not seem fair that athletes should be held hostage in a project that is about protecting children and young people against making unhealthy choices. As mentioned, we do not prohibit other role models like musicians or parents from drinking alcohol or smoking tobacco. And with good reason. It would be extremely difficult and expensive to enforce such a prohibition. Add to this that enforcing such a prohibition would constantly infringe on the individual person's freedom in a way that would probably hurt many people's lives.

Doping and my children

The concern for young people can also be expressed without wrapping it in role model attire. In interviews and at conferences, I have often been asked the following question when I have argued that WADA's prohibited list is too extensive:

> Would you want your children to use substances from WADA's doping list? Would you want your children to use EPO or blood doping? What would you say if your children chose a sport where they would have to dope to be in the elite?

The questions, as I see them, are an attempt to convince the counterparty that if you do *not* want your children to use substances or methods from the prohibited list, *then* use of doping should remain prohibited.

It generally seems like a very safe and sympathetic moral principle that the actions we do not want our children to engage in should also be illegal. All good parents want their children to have a good life.

And a good starting point for a serious debate is to investigate whether you are willing to accept the consequences your positions have on those you care the most about – typically your children. But on second thoughts, it is a problematic line of thought. Try, for instance, to consider the consequences of this line of thought.

There are naturally many actions we do not want our children to engage in. To be quite honest, I do not want my children to go to boxing, ballroom dancing or motor sports. I think it is either too dangerous or too expensive, and there are other alternatives that are just as good at developing my children socially and physically. But just because I have this prejudice, it does not make it a good argument for making ballroom dancing illegal.

Allow me to present another example that clearly shows that simply because you want your children not to engage in a specific action, it does not mean that actions should be prohibited. My own parents did not want me and my wife to take a three-week trip to Indonesia with our children some 15 years ago. Both my parents thought that it sounded dangerous with the terrorism that at this time affected a very small part of the region, a region that were situated far away from where we should stay. But it would not be a substantial argument for deeming family travels of this type immoral or perhaps making them illegal and punishable! The correlation between what we want for our children and what should be illegal is very arbitrary and may have unreasonable consequences since many so-called normal and morally unproblematic actions would then become illegal.

I can now conclude that the role model argument for the current doping policy should be given the red card. There is no scientific evidence indicating that children and young people use doping simply because their idols do. Even if a correlation exists between role model's use of doping and young people's use of doping, then – as described in Chapter 1 – there are good reason to believe that it would be less harmful with a regulated and white market for doping than the current prohibition policy. A documented correlation between adults' use of legal doping and children's use of illegal doping would obviously be problematic and would warrant action. An action resembling the one taken when it comes to alcohol and young people. An action where we (the health authorities, parents, teachers, etc.) inform about the dangers of drinking alcohol. An action where it is illegal to sell alcohol to children, but where it is still legal to sell it to adults. The same action should be applied to doping.

Notes

1 Mikkelsen (2003).
2 CNN. https://edition.cnn.com/2009/US/02/01/michael.phelps.marijuana/ (accessed March 18, 2020).
3 Tamburrini (2000).
4 In the following, I will use the word 'children' about people under the age of 18 and the word 'young people' about people aged 18–23.
5 For a short description of the various role model arguments, see, e.g. Petersen (2010).
6 See, e.g. Miller et al. (2002) and Beamish (2009).

4   Doping and coercion

Helena, an American elite marathon runner, who I spoke to at a conference on ethics and sport, expressed why she is against allowing doping:

> If doping is legalised, most athletes will use performance enhancing drugs in connection with my sport. So if I want to be part of the elite, I will also be coerced to use such drugs. But I want to participate in a doping-free elite sport and do not want to be forced to risk my health in connection with my sport.

Helena told me that she felt compelled to use legal performance-enhancing supplements such as creatine and protein powder because she knew that her competitors used those supplements. Helena's point was that we should have a very restrictive doping policy banning doping. If doping was not banned, then athletes who want to compete at the highest level would be coerced to use doping. That type of coercion would, according to Helena, also have negative health consequences for her. In Chapter 1, we discussed whether the potentially harmful consequences of using doping can be used as a good argument in favour of the current doping policy. In this chapter, I will focus on the part of Helena's argument that concerns the ethical aspects of whether allowing doping would result in coercion for the athletes who do not want to use doping. In other words, I want to ask: Will allowing doping result in coerced doping and thereby violate the autonomy of the athletes?

But before we answer that question, I would like to emphasise why this argument is important and then describe what kind of coercion Helena and others express when they claim that legalised doping would coerce athletes to use doping. There are several reasons why this argument plays an important part in the discussion of where to draw the line for the use of doping.

First, it is reasonable to assume that the autonomy or self-determination of the athletes is a key ethical value worth safeguarding. So if allowing certain types of doping violates the autonomy of athletes, then that speaks against allowing doping. Second, it is rather thought-provoking in this connection that a central argument in favour of allowing athletes to use doping reaches the opposite conclusion of what Helena believes. Namely that we respect the autonomy of the athletes with regard to whether or not they want to use doping if using doping was allowed. In this context, the argument is that adults, rational and well-informed individuals, have the right to decide what they want to expose themselves to. Other people should not decide what the athlete should do to his/her body – that is up to the athlete. But if Helena and others are right in claiming that access to doping violates the autonomy of the athletes, then they also contribute to undermining one of the most central arguments in favour of athletes' access to doping. And that is the reason why this argument plays a key role in our debate.

Helena explained to me that the type of coercion she was talking about was not a type of coercion where she personally would be physically forced against her will to use doping. Force-fed doping is a clear example of what we call brute force or *direct coercion*. However, according to Helena, another type of coercion than the direct coercion exists which we should not neglect in an ethical discussion. Helena believed that the fact that her competitors would use doping, if the doping rules were substantially relaxed, would coerce her to use doping if she wanted to be part of the elite. Because if she does not use doping and her competitors do, then Helena will never win. And the fact that she is subjected to that type of coercion will undermine her autonomy. Or in other words: Her possibility of realising her wish to participate and compete in a doping-free elite sport will be swept away. Let us call this type of coercion which, according to Helena, affects her autonomy negatively *indirect coercion*. Helena is not the only one with this objection.[1] For example, American professor of sports, Warren Fraleigh, states that allowing doping would mean "... that athletes will be forced to self-harm".[2] And Holowchak, American professor of philosophy, states that a ban against anabolic steroids "... supports autonomy rather than destroys autonomy...".[3]

However, I believe – not very surprisingly – that this objection is questionable for several reasons. But before any criticism is made of this objection, it is important that the following is crystal clear: If athletes are subjected to *direct coercion* in connection with the use of doping, it is obviously morally reprehensible. A clarification of 'direct coercion' in our context would be if an athlete is physically restrained and force-fed doping against her will. This type of coercion is indisputably immoral as it violates the autonomy of the athletes and is an expression of violence. However, when athletes are doped, it is typically not through the use of direct coercion.

Do you think that great sport personalities such as the tennis player Maria Sharapova or Lance Armstrong were directly coerced against their will to use doping? Hardly. An athlete can typically say no to performing his/her sport and can refuse to use doping too. Moreover, legalising doping does not mean passivity in relation to preventing situations where the autonomy of athletes is in fact violated. Legalising doping is fully compatible with simultaneous extensive enforcement of rules protecting the autonomy of the athletes against direct coercion. It might, of course, be a cause for concern that totalitarian states would subject their athletes to direct coercion. However, although the risk of technology abuse (such as television, Internet, medicine and doping) is greater in totalitarian states, we should not combat the use of such technologies. Instead, I suggest that we combat the totalitarian regimes and their abuse of technology. No one would think that we should ban the use of television and Internet in general just because television and Internet is abused in totalitarian states.

However, although direct physical coercion is generally not seen in connection with doping, there might be some indirect coercion without the use of violence. This obviously depends on what we mean by the term 'indirect coercion'. One way of defining indirect coercion is the following: If a person A subjects a person B to indirect coercion, the following three conditions must be met[4]:

- A wants to make B do X
- A communicates a requirement to B
- A's requirement is that if B fails to do X, then it will have some consequences that will make B worse off than if B does X.

Let us first look into whether it makes sense to say that allowing doping would in itself result in indirect coercion. If a sports federation or anti-doping organisation decides to legalise a number of doping drugs, then none of the three conditions for indirect coercion are met.

First: If WADA (World Anti-Doping Agency) decides to remove EPO and anabolic steroids from their prohibited list, this does not in itself express a wish for the athletes to use doping. When WADA removed caffeine from their prohibited list in 2004, the reason was that caffeine was not significantly performance enhancing and that the presence of caffeine in many food products made it difficult to distinguish between normal and excessive use of caffeine. The reason for removing caffeine from the prohibited list was not a wish to have more athletes drink caffeinated beverages, such as coffee or energy drinks, or to make them eat more chocolate. Permitting a drug is not the same as urging athletes to use it. The fact that I believe that tobacco should be permitted is fully compatible with my view that for health reasons, no one should smoke tobacco, and that we should implement political measures making it difficult to buy tobacco or smoke tobacco. For example, by raising the price of tobacco and banning smoking in all cafes and pubs. So, this means that the first condition for indirect coercion is not met. WADA can lift the ban doping without urging the athletes to do anything in particular.

Second: It seems reasonable to assume that if WADA, for instance, remove EPO from the prohibited list, they do not demand anything from the athletes.

And third: WADA does not put athletes who do not use EPO in bad standing, e.g. by punishing them.

So if WADA removes certain drugs from the prohibited list, this will, according to the above analysis, not be indirect coercion as none of the three conditions for coercion are met. If my analysis is true, then it undermines the idea that allowing certain doping drugs would result in coercion and thereby also violate the autonomy of the athletes.

However, if a sports manager or coach wants her athlete to use doping and states that the condition for the athlete to be on the team or going to the Olympics is that she uses doping, then evidently, it is indirect coercion. But the big question is whether the coach in the above situations is acting immorally?

The way I see it, that depends on two conditions. Is it necessary for the coach to demand that the athlete use doping in order to perform satisfactorily, and what are the negative consequences for the athlete if she does not do what the coach wants? A coach will always demand something from his/her athletes and that in itself is not immoral. Yet in the above example, I think that the coach is doing something which is morally wrong. What every coach should ensure is that the athletes are doing well and that the athletes develop their potential. The coach can say that if the athlete does not stick to her training plan and underperforms at competitions, then she will not go to the Olympics.

That is morally fine. But the way for the athlete to achieve those results should be discussed with the coach who may suggest doping as a possibility, but not a requirement for going to the Olympics. The most important thing is that the athlete is doing well and performs optimally and not that the coach requires the athlete to use doping if she wants to go to the Olympics. So, morally speaking, it is not fair that the coach demands that the athlete use doping, but it is fair to say that if the athlete does not perform satisfactorily, then she will not be on the Olympic team.

But again, if the coach threatens the athlete that her family will be killed if she does not use doping, then obviously, it is morally wrong. With such a threat, the athlete is left with no choice. The negative consequences of saying no to doping are so devastating that the athlete is directly coerced to use doping. So, things are somewhat complicated when it comes to the moral assessment of indirect coercion. But perhaps we can interpret the concerns that Helena and other people have with regard to doping and coercion in a slightly more compassionate light. Instead of speaking about direct or indirect coercion, it might be more correct to say that removing certain drugs from the prohibited list will result in a *social pressure* to use doping. A morally problematic pressure from the surroundings, which has negative consequences for the athletes who do not want to use doping. A social pressure which will occur because the athlete knows that all her competitors are probably using doping. So let us replace 'coercion' by 'social pressure'.

However, this change of words means that the argument loses some of its power. One thing is to directly coerce people to do something they do not want to do or use heavy-handed threats. A completely different thing is to experience a social pressure to use doping because other people are doing so. Or to experience a social pressure because friends and acquaintances try to convince you to think something different or do something else than what you are used to. If we were not allowed to try to pressure people by means of, e.g. arguments to think something else than what they do, the freedom of speech would be hard to maintain. And if we zoom back to the world of sports, this mind-set is also a problem.

If we accept that the pressure from other athletes to perform better at competitions is an expression of a morally problematic pressure, then it has unreasonable consequences. According to this mind-set, it would, e.g. be an unreasonable pressure for a marathon runner to feel forced to train twice a day to be able to compete with the other marathon runners. Of course it might be a problematic psychological pressure for the individual to perform her best and having to train twice a day. But this is not a morally problematic pressure. Nobody would consider the requirements for elite sports as immoral simply because the athlete experiences a pressure to perform her best and train several times a day. In elite sports, it is a well-known fact, and as a former elite athlete I know by heart, that in order to be at the top level, you have to train just as hard or even harder or smarter than your competitors. And then also renounce alcohol, tobacco, junk food and partying.

I generally believe that it is reasonable to expect that a person chooses to become an athlete and that a person chooses whether or not to use doping. Athletes often make voluntary choices in relation to their sporting life, also in connection with doping. And that is supported by the fact that we already accept that athletes choose themselves whether they want to follow a training programme, participate in a tournament, take medicine which is not on WADA's prohibited list, renounce the use of alcohol and tobacco, postpone education, etc. If we trust that athletes are free to choose in those situations, then why not believe that they can decide on an informed basis whether or not they want to use doping? Obviously an athlete might in special cases be under pressure, e.g. from a trainer, to use doping. This scenario is, as already mentioned, morally problematic and should not take place. Yet generally, we must assume that athletes, at least in non-totalitarian countries, are in a position to decide whether or not they want to use doping. Given that they are, of course, well informed about what effects and side effects it may have to use doping and that the drugs and their use are within some established safety values and that the athletes are monitored by sports physicians for health reasons.

This mind-set goes well with our actions within a number of areas other than sports. In the health sector, we also accept that people refrain from treatment although the physician knows that it might be very harmful to the health to refuse treatment. The basis for such acceptance is that we assume that it is a voluntary and well-informed decision made by a rational individual. Let me give another example. As a university teacher, I generally assume that the students I teach and supervise are able to choose whether they want to continue their studies (I will, of course, serve as a mentor for students who are in doubt). Like many athletes, the students are under pressure as their quality of life and financial situation also partly depend on the study programme they choose and whether they perform well academically during their studies. But the fact that some circumstances may pressure the students to act in a certain way does not mean that the 'pressuring' framework for their decisions is necessarily ethically problematic.

Being under moderate pressure or influence to perform your best also has positive consequences. It may help you perform better and learn more than if there were no pressure. If we should not accept any pressure at all, the consequence would be that we had to close all educational institutions and sports clubs. But nobody would think that.

So, we have to learn to live with a certain amount of pressure to perform, whether the pressure comes from the surroundings or ourselves. Finally, I would like to point out another two challenges for Helena's concern that the autonomy of athletes is undermined if we allow a number of doping drugs.

First: The current doping ban is also some kind of coercion for athletes who want to use toping. They are punished if they use doping. A consequence of this observation is that regardless of whether we have a ban or not, there will always be some athletes who feel that they are subject to coercion. So if we believe that autonomy is a key value, we should consider the fact than on second thought, a ban will not necessarily increase the autonomy of athletes. This depends on whether there are more athletes who want a number of drugs from the prohibited list, such as EPO and testosterone, to be legalised than the number of athletes who do not want any of these drugs to be legalised. However, as far as I know, no large studies have yet been made to clarify the views of the athletes in the above; we still do not know enough about whether a relaxation of the rules would increase or decrease the autonomy of athletes.

Second, I am also sceptical when it comes to Helena's concern that allowing certain doping drugs would force athletes who do not want to use doping not to compete in sports at the highest elite level. For example, some athletes are so genetically blessed that nature has provided them with a large number of oxygen-carrying red blood cells or with more and faster muscle fibres than most other athletes. Such athletes would probably be able to compete on equal terms with doped athletes.

But even if doped athletes often would perform better than non-doped athletes, it would still be possible to compete at a high elite level without using doping. If doping were allowed, it would be possible to make some divisions or distinctions in the different sports disciplines that would make it possible even for non-doped athletes to compete at the highest level. We already divide the individual sports into different categories. In cycling and many other sports disciplines, the participants are already classified by their age, gender and whether the athletes in, for instance, para-cycling use a hand cycle or a tandem bike. The same idea can be applied to distinguish between doped and non-doped athletes. If we make such classification, it will still be possible for non-doped athletes to participate in elite sports for non-doped athletes.

I can now conclude that if doping is allowed, it does not mean that athletes will be coerced to use doping. But if athletes are subjected to direct coercion or threats to life if they do not use doping, this is obviously immoral. Athletes might, of course, feel the pressure from their competitors to use doping if doping were allowed. But this is not necessarily a moral problem. I sometimes feel pressured into doing lots of things. This could be in connection with certain tasks at work or the fact that I take care to be polite to the people I meet. But it seems out of proportion to think that I am automatically subject to a morally problematic pressure in those situations. And even if I agreed that a relaxation of the rules might result in indirect coercion, we must not forget that the current rules also force the athletes who want to use doping away from having autonomy over their own body. Finally, it is far from obvious that allowing doping would mean that athletes could not compete at top level. Some athletes are born with major genetic advantages, and a possibility could be to divide sports into competitions where doping was allowed and competitions where doping was not allowed.

Notes

1 See, e.g. Murray (1983), Holowchak (2000) and Petersen and Kristensen (2009). For a critical discussion of the objection, see Veber (2014).
2 Fraleigh (1985, p. 28).
3 Holowchak (2000).
4 This definition is inspired by Nozick (1969).

5 Doping and the wish for prohibition

One apparently strong argument in favour of WADA's doping policy builds on the premise that the majority of athletes wants doping to be prohibited. In other words: We should uphold the prohibition against doping because it will mean that we respect the athletes' wish for a doping-free sport.

However, before I reconstruct and criticise this argument, I would like to weed out any obvious criticism of the argument, which states that simply because a majority believes or wants something it does not have to be morally right. Many used to believe that the Earth was flat or that women were inferior. But as we all know, they were wrong. So, for obvious reasons, the majority's idea of what the world looks or should look like is not infallible. We should therefore demand a good argument for the current doping policy instead of merely referring to what a possible majority of athletes might want. So is there any good reason for a majority of athletes wanting a prohibition against doping? We can apply game theory to find a rational reason for why most athletes might want a doping ban.[1] The principal idea behind the above argument is that it would be the most rational for all athletes if they could compete in a world where doping was prohibited. In the following, I will first try to describe this argument in detail and in the strongest version possible. Then, the argument will be subjected to criticism, and I will argue that it would be most rational if the athletes wanted to live in a world where the current prohibition against doping was lifted.

What should the rational athlete choose?

Assume that two racing cyclists, Maria and Nina, have to choose between the following four scenarios:

1   Both use doping

    If both Maria and Nina use doping, then, all else being equal, they should have the same chance of winning.[2] But let us also assume that they both want to accept the additional health risk of using doping. Consider also that Maria and Nina will incur additional costs since they will have to spend time and money on doping. In this situation, *neither* of the two racing cyclist would benefit from using doping. The benefits they might achieve by using doping would be evened out by the fact that they both use doping. Furthermore, they would both incur additional costs by having to spend resources on buying and spending time on using doping.

2   Both do not use doping

    If neither Maria nor Nina uses doping, then, all else being equal, they should have the same chance of winning. Both racing cyclists would be better off in this scenario than in the former because neither of them would run the additional health risk of using doping, and neither of them would have to spend time and money on using doping.

3   Maria uses doping while Nina does not

    If Maria uses doping and Nina does not, Nina would have an advantage in terms of health. However, the chance of Nina winning against Maria is small. This scenario would be best for Maria given that the health risk is trumped by the benefit of winning more often than Nina.

4   Nina uses doping while Maria does not

    If Nina uses doping and Maria does not, Maria would have an advantage in terms of health. However, the chance of Maria winning against Nina is small. This scenario would be best for Nina given that the health risk is trumped by the benefit of winning more often than Maria.

But what would be the most rational choice for Maria and Nina? On the face of it, the third scenario would be the best for Maria, as she would gain a major competitive edge compared to her competitors. The same applies to Nina in regard to the fourth scenario. Conversely, the fourth scenario would be the least optimum for Maria as would the third scenario for Nina. However, there are good ethical reasons for writing off the third and fourth scenarios.

First, both scenarios are unfair. It seems extremely difficult to provide a good reason for why it should only be Maria (third scenario), who can use doping, or why it should only be Nina (fourth scenario), who can use doping. We should assume that there are no relevant differences between Maria and Nina that can justify treating Maria's and Nina's doping use differently.[3]

Second, it seems unrealistic that the third and fourth scenarios would be accepted by a democratically elected sports organisation or a majority of athletes. Accordingly, the best bid for a realistic doping policy that rational athletes would choose must be the ones presented in the first and second scenarios. Doping for both or no doping at all.

If the descriptions of these two scenarios are correct, it seems most rational for Maria and Nina (and all other athletes) that they can compete in a world where doping is prohibited. That would be the most rational choice, since both racing cyclists would be better off in the second scenario than in the first. In other words, the conclusion is that the apparently most rational and most fair and realistic path would be to uphold the current prohibition or a similar prohibition against doping. However, I intend to show that this way of thinking comes with some challenges. Challenges so serious that we have to reject the argument. I want to show that the most rational wish for the athletes would be a change of the current doping rules to allow a wide range of doping substances and methods. Meaning that rational athletes like Maria and Nina should choose the first scenario.

Doping is rational

Let us start by noting that the central assumption in the description of all four scenarios, namely that doping is harmful, is wrong. As I outlined in detail in Chapter 1, the use of performance-enhancing drugs on the anti-doping organisations' prohibited list can be beneficial for health as they can help prevent diseases. Or there are a wide range of substances and methods that are not harmful to use under the proper medical conditions. Substances like testosterone and EPO can help improve and shorten the recovery of a body that has been broken down by extreme sport activity and thus help strengthen the athlete's immune system. In addition, WADA's list of prohibited substances and methods includes substances and methods that are not harmful. Examples include use of intravenous administration of water, glucose, minerals and salts. In fact, the use of intravenous administration of salts and minerals may help improve and shorten the recovery of athletes, whose bodies are physically exhausted due to intense training or competition.

Finally, Chapter 1 also clarifies that even if using doping is harmful or constitutes a risk to athlete's health, the same would apply to most sports as well as alcohol and tobacco. Yet, few believe that it should be a criminal offence to do sport, smoke tobacco or drink alcohol even though these activities can be harmful. Furthermore, it was remarkable that we were unable to identify any good reasons for the view: That one harmful act (doping) was morally more wrong than another (sport, tobacco, alcohol). However, if you believe that it is a problem that doping is harmful but are still willing to accept that elite sport is harmful, then it would be equally rational to choose either the first or second scenario. In the first scenario, you would naturally have to spend time and money on doping compared to the second scenario. However, allowing doping as in the first scenario would, as we have seen, also have some health benefits that may very well trump the time and money spent on doping.

In respect of the above scenarios, it is also a problematic assumption that the most important value of using doping is that you are put at an advantage compared to your competitors. At an advantage because the chance of winning against them is greater if you use doping than if you do not. Doping is then perceived as a *positional good*.[4] This means a good that is only good to have if others do not also have it. For instance, it is a positional good to be two metres tall if you are at a no-seating music festival. Here, it is a good being two metres tall, because you will be able to see the musicians on stage much better than people of average height. However, being two metres tall would stop being a good at a music festival if everyone at the festival was the same height.

However, I believe that doping is not just a positional good where it is only an advantage to use doping if others do not use doping. Doping can be a good capable of enriching and improving the athlete's quality of life irrespective of whether others use doping. First, as just illustrated, use of doping can be healthy and help improve the athlete's immune system after intense sport activity. This is essential to the athlete's quality of life and health in the both short and long terms.

Second, an athlete can choose to use doping because it satisfies some wishes that do not hinge on the comparison with other athletes. For instance, use of doping can help you do more of the things you like to do. It might be that you love to train and become able to train more or more efficiently by using doping than if you do not use doping. Or it might be that you can set a personal record or get the kind of muscle definition you desire, which, in turn, contributes to your quality of life. But if the athletes use of doping is not just a positional good, it suggests that the first scenario where everyone uses (or can use) doping is better than the second scenario where no one use doping.

A third assumption that supports the rationality of athletes choosing the first scenario is that it is what the athletes actually want. However, it is more difficult to answer whether it is true that the athletes want a doping-free sport. Though, we could start by acknowledging the fact that doping actually takes place and that many athletes worldwide use or have used doping. The fact that athletes use doping shows that they to some extent accept the use of doping. This may be because they believe that it is not harmful or because they are convinced that it can actually be healthy to use certain types of doping. Or it may be because they believe that it is rational to use doping since the doping control is inefficient. The doping control will always have limited resources at its disposal, meaning that many athletes go untested. Moreover, it is possible to dope using substances and methods that are extremely difficult to detect – like blood doping with your own blood. Or it may be because the athletes believe that it is morally acceptable that an adult, well-informed person exposes him-/herself to a risk of harm. This might be a risk associated with a specific substance or participating in a dangerous sport like boxing or motor sports. So the number of athletes wanting to keep the current doping policy may prove not to be a majority.

To counterbalance the observations that say that it is rational to use doping, it could be noted that many athletes have publicly spoken against doping. However, such statements should, as a minimum, be taken with a grain of salt.

First, many athletes have been outspoken opponents of doping and have explicitly said that they have not used doping, only to be tested positive or admitting to using doping. Former elite racing cyclists like Lance Armstrong and Bjarne Riis as well as British athlete and winner of Olympic gold in 100 metres (1992), Linford Christie, have all been outspoken and high-profiled opponents of doping. However, that was before they all tested positive for doping or admitted to having used doping.

Second, it comes at a great cost to criticise the current doping policy and probably at an even greater cost to speak in favour of doping. If an athlete speaks in favour of doping, he or she will probably get the cold shoulder from coaches, sports organisations and sponsors. So any criticism of the current doping rules is quelled early on. Not because of good arguments but because the price is too high. Furthermore, it is worth noting that the basic notion that it is the active athletes who want doping to be prohibited is highly inconsistent with *who* has actually argued for, introduced and made the doping rules. It was the International Olympic Committee (IOC) and the European Commission that made doping policy decisions at the beginning of the 1960s – not the athletes.[5]

Third, there is every reason to be sceptical of statements made by athletes when they claim that doping should be prohibited. Athletes who use doping benefit from arguing that the substances they use should remain prohibited. Because, if doping was allowed, they would not benefit as much from it, since all other athletes would be able to use doping without the risk of getting caught. So game theory provides good reasons for believing that there is no correlation between what the athlete says and what he/she actually thinks of doping.

Finally: Even if people could *agree* that use of doping is immoral and should be prohibited, such agreement is untenable. Indeed, such agreement is threatened by the fact that we do not always act in accordance with our moral outlook. It is unlikely that all athletes would act in accordance with their moral outlook, since a prohibition against doping would make it rational to use doping provided that the risk of getting caught is small and the benefit of using doping is high. So, again, there are good reasons for not attaching too much importance to athletes' (erratic) outlook on doping.[6]

The past 50 years' doping policy shows in no uncertain terms that the second scenario above is utopian and that it would be most rational to choose the first scenario. The current doping policy is utopian because doping is here to stay, and athletes will always use doping since so few get caught and the benefit is great and there will always be types of doping that are too elusive to test for. Moreover, the funds for doping tests are limited, leading to inadequate resources for enforcing the prohibition.

The conclusion is therefore that it would be more rational to allow doping for all instead of having a situation like now where some take the chance and use doping while others do not. A new doping policy like the one I'm proposing would be more rational, improve health and create greater transparency in sport and – as I will explain in the next chapter – a fairer competition. The concern that the use of doping prevents fair competition between athletes is the topic of the next chapter.

Notes

1 Broadly speaking, game theory is about answering the following question: What should a *rational agent* do – i.e. an agent who wants to maximise the things he or she finds valuable and realistic to execute – when the agent's actions depend on what others would do? For a short introduction to game theory, see, e.g. Binmore (2007).

2 I say 'all else being equal' since there are many factors that determine who will win a competition. These include talent, training, genetics, fitness on the day, mental strength, the right equipment, luck, etc.
3 See, e.g. Breivik (1987).
4 See, e.g. Bostrom and Roache (2008).
5 Møller (2010, p. 42).
6 In discussing this objection, I have primarily drawn inspiration from Tamburrini (2000, p. 214).

6   Doping and fair competition

The idea that fairness dictates that athletes should have equal opportunities to perform their best, and that permitting doping prevents the realisation of this fairness ideal, is quite common.[1] Take the view of Morten Mølholm, Director of the Sports Confederation of Denmark and Olympic Secretary General in the Danish Olympic Committee. He thinks doping should be banned because:

> The competitive element of sport is linked to the notion of competition between equal athletes, who have had the same opportunities to prepare themselves and to perform. This notion of fairness is lost when some athletes acquire a competitive edge by using illegal substances. [my translation].[2]

Another example is WADA which declares that "[t]he purposes of the World Anti-Doping Program and the Code are: To protect the Athletes' fundamental right to participate in doping-free sport and thus promote health, fairness and equality for Athletes worldwide ...".[3] In addition, one of the ways in which WADA believes it promotes fairness for athletes is by banning certain substances and methods and by punishing those who do dope. Also, WADA's Ethics Panel alludes to the value of fairness when they state:

> Fairness and Justice: Although individuals are fundamentally different and not equal, and the circumstances under which athletes might have to train are not the same (e.g. due to differences in resources), efforts should be made in sport to provide equal opportunity and to facilitate fair competition.[4]

In Chapter 1, I argued that the use of doping can be in keeping with protecting the athletes' health. So we need not address WADA's purpose of promoting the athletes' health in this chapter. Instead, I will address the other values stated in the quote from Morten Mølholm above and in WADA's statement of purpose: That doping is unfair and creates inequality among athletes.

Before criticising this way of reasoning, I would like to make it clear that it can be difficult to distinguish between the concepts 'unfair' and 'inequality'. At first glance, the two concepts look like synonyms. Indeed, in many situations, if an action is described as unfair then it would also constitute a morally problematic inequality. If a football player, for instances, scores a goal with his hand and the referee does not see it, most would feel that it is unfair and against the rules. But an unfair goal with the hand (the hand of God maybe!) can also result in morally problematic inequality. If the goal scored with the hand is decisive for the outcome of the match, it would be reasonable to think that it is the unfair act that leads to inequality between the winning and losing team, which is morally problematic. The same applies if you use doping against the rules and it means that you win against a person who is not doped.

However, in other situations, the two concepts are not the same. There are many examples in sport where inequality does not always lead to unfairness. I think that most would find that inequality in terms of the height of basketball players is not the kind of inequality that would be considered unfair in sport. In criticising the viewpoint that the current doping policy is morally right because it protects athletes against unfairness and inequality, I do not want to complicate matters further by engaging in a lengthy discussion of the fact that 'unfairness' and 'inequality' can have different meanings. The thing that I believe that Mølholm and WADA focus on in their defence of anti-doping is the simple idea that doping prevents athletes from competing equally with each other, in the sense of following the rules of the game. In other words, use of doping is inconsistent with fair competition.

However, as I mentioned in the introduction, it is obvious that if the athletes violate the rules of sport, then we cannot have a fair competition. So the use of doping in a world of sports that has rules against doping is evidently cheating and thus unfair. So far, Mølholm and WADA is right. It is unfair to use doping because it violates rules that apply to all. However, this line of thinking presumes that doping is morally wrong. Believing that it is cheating, unfair or unjust to use doping is not a good argument for prohibiting doping per se. The key thing is to determine what actions we want to characterise as cheating or as being unfair or unjust and why we believe that these actions are so immoral that they should be punishable.

The fundamental notion of this book is that, although doping at present is cheating because it violates the rules and therefore is morally wrong, we should change the rules so that it would not be cheating to use doping substances and methods within certain limits. And as I try to demonstrate throughout this book: Since there are no good reasons for having certain substances and methods on WADA's prohibited list, it should be allowed to use them.

But a central question is: If we allow doping, would it then be reasonable to think that it would undermine fair competition? Or put differently, would it be unfair or increase inequality among athletes to compete for titles, records and honour if doping was allowed and would then not constitute cheating? Generally, I intend to argue that, on closer inspection, the praised notion of fair competition, which is central to the ideal of sport, is far-fetched. WADA and Mølholm are voicing a sympathetic ideal. An ideal that is impossible to live up to in practice. Most sport events do not come through as fair, quite the contrary. In the world of sports, we praise and celebrate the individuals who have won in the genetic and social lottery (I will explain this in the next section); a lottery that no athlete can control. I will also argue that by allowing certain types of doping, we can increase equality among athletes in the sense that they will be able to compete on more equal terms than when doping is prohibited. But first, I will describe why sport is not an expression of fair competition between athletes.

Sport is not fair – about the genetic and social lottery

Despite rules being a condition for fair competition, it is hardly correct when Mølholm – says that competitive sport builds on "... competition between equal athletes, who have had the same opportunities of preparing themselves and performing"?

An athlete who does well in sports is often the product of random factors that the athlete has not had to work for. Perhaps the athlete is equipped in a way by nature that means that she does well in a given sport. Normally, we would say that it is unfair that persons who are well equipped by nature in terms of, e.g. muscle mass, height, speed, endurance, mental strength should receive honour and money. Instead, we should support persons who at no fault of their own are not as fortunate. Why should people who are over two metres tall have a clear advantage in terms of earning money on playing basketball, while a shorter person has virtually no chance of becoming a professional basketball player? But that is exactly what sport, among other things, helps support. Elite sport supports giving extra advantages to persons who are already at an advantage.

It is therefore reasonable to point out that sport as currently practised in most fields does not constitute fair competition in the sense promoted by Mølholm. Indeed, sport will probably never be fair as envisioned by Mølholm, since it is practically impossible to compensate fully for inequalities between athletes who are a product of their genetics. So we can conclude that sport is basically unfair since genetic factors that you have not had to work for are decisive for whether you do well in sport. Elite sport celebrates and pays the genetically fortunate and largely excludes persons who, genetically speaking, stand no chance of succeeding in elite sport.

However, becoming a top athlete takes more than winning in the genetic lottery. You should ideally also win in the social lottery. It is a fact that the best athletes in many sports typically come from families that are well-off or from rich countries, or from an elite in a poor country.[5] You can be extremely talented and still never get the opportunity to win an Olympic medal if you grow up in a country without access to good training facilities, skilled trainers and resources for participating in international competitions. Except unless you are a poor athlete who is headhunted by talent scouts from a rich club or a wealthy country. Sports economic studies indicate that an Olympic gold medal costs around USD 32 million.[6] It is therefore reasonable to point out again that sport as practised in most fields is unfair. And sport is unfair because social factors that you have not had to work for are decisive for whether you do well in sport.

In response to my objections, you could say that the athletes deserve to win because they work and train hard. However, this is quickly countered. First, being able to train hard and live ascetically probably also comes down to genetic factors. Genetic factors that make it easier to deal with mental and physically strenuous training and be content with an ascetic lifestyle. Second: If you do not have the financial means and access to skilled trainers and good training facilities, then you can work as hard as you like, you will still not be able to become an elite athlete.

So persons who are well equipped by nature and born with social advantages have the best opportunities of winning in the world of sports and being rewarded with honour and prize money. Sport is therefore a practice that unequivocally supports a 'survival of the fittest and richest' mentality. All the while, athletes who use doping to compensate for their shortcomings because they lost out in the genetic or social lottery are punished, ridiculed and stigmatised. But why not celebrate the fairness of an athlete trying to compensate for his/her lack of natural abilities or social background by using doping (provided that doping is allowed)? A counterargument could be that this will not increase fairness since the athletes who have won in the genetic and social lottery will also use doping. However, these athletes have, all else being equal, less of an incentive to dope, if they, by nature, are already close to the safety values (e.g. a haematocrit values of 50%), that I and others believe should apply to a new doping policy. And if tests show that the values exceed the allowed values, they will not be allowed to compete.

It is odd that we despite this will not accept doping, when we in other parts of society are willing to accept that persons with disabilities use drugs and aids to compensate for poor vision, hearing or organ failure. The explanation of this difference is, as I have previously shown in my ethical analysis of arguments against allowing doping, the result of sloppy thinking. Sport is not and cannot be fair. We should stop talking about sport as a generally fair competition. Instead, we should reserve the ideal of fair competition for when we observe that a set of common rules for what we want competitive sport to be about are not violated. However, as I will show in the next section, allowing doping can help increase the athletes' chances of competing on more equal terms than is the case with the current doping rules. So even though absolute equality among athletes is not possible due to the genetic and social lottery, I will show that a relaxation of the doping rules *can* also help increase equality among athletes.

Allowed doping can create fair competition

But can allowed doping really help increase the chance of fair competition between athletes? It's an open question if you ask me. But unfortunately a question that is rarely asked or answered. So let me give it a go.

On the one hand, a relaxation of WADA's extensive doping list – which will probably mean that drugs will play a greater role for the athletes' performance than today – would do nothing to improve the position of poor athletes. In fact they would be worse off than today, because drugs and methods, in combination with counselling and treatment by sport physicians, are often costly. On the other hand, it is far from certain that the inequality between rich and poor athletes will increase if doping is allowed.

First, today, the athletes who use doping and can afford to consult expensive and skilled sport physicians have a much greater chance of not being tested positive for doping than poor athletes, who use doping, but who do not have access to expensive and skilled doctors who can manage the use of doping, so that it cannot be detected. This inequality would not exist if doping was allowed.

Second, by allowing a substance like EPO, we would give athletes a better chance of competing on equal terms. Paradoxically, the prohibition against EPO increases the *inequality* among athletes. It increases inequality in terms of having access to increase the number of red blood cells (which is what EPO is used for). Allow me to explain why the prohibition against EPO increases inequality among athletes. The status quo is as follows:

- Some athletes use EPO, others are afraid of using it out of fear of getting ill or caught and punished.
- Genetically, humans differ in terms of how many red blood cells they have. Some humans (around 5%) have around 40% more red blood cells than normal humans.[7] Finnish cross-country skier Eero Mäntyranta, who won two gold medals at the 1964 Olympics in Innsbruck, is a good example of this genetic inequality that exists among athletes. Because of a genetic mutation, Mäntyranta had about 40% more red blood cells than an average athlete.
- Some athletes increase their number of red blood cells by doing altitude training several weeks during the year at training facilities that lie higher than 2,000 metres above sea level. Other athletes increase the number of red blood cells by sleeping in oxygen tents, using an altitude generator or using an altitude house. All these methods are legal as they are not listed on WADA's prohibited list. Yet some athletes do not have these opportunities as they are extremely expensive.

So is the current situation fair to the athletes? No. But we can make it fairer by lifting the ban on medical EPO. The genetic difference in the number of red blood cells the athletes have can be evened out or reduced by allowing EPO. And since EPO only costs around USD 150[8] per month and therefore is much cheaper to use than, for instance, an altitude house or an oxygen tent, it will make it possible for more athletes to increase their number of red blood cells. It is often very expensive to train in high-altitude areas. Particularly if they lie far away from where you live. An altitude house is not cheap either and costs around USD 45,000, while an altitude generator costs around USD 3,800.[9] Sports organisations can help ensure that inequality among athletes does not grow bigger than it is today by making performance-enhancing drugs and methods available to the athletes. Such a strategy would largely resemble the way in which various sports associations and organisations help their best athletes by making facilities and equipment available for free or by fully or partially financing training camps, paying for tournament fees, etc.

I hope to have shown that it is clearly cheating and therefore immoral to use doping if you as an athlete accept to compete under democratically adopted rules. Moreover, I have accepted that the idea that competition between athletes is only fair if the athletes have the same opportunities to prepare and perform. But this viewpoint is also practically impossible to live up to and therefore comes off as far-fetched. Instead, WADA's viewpoint is that we should strive to give athletes the same conditions even though we know that they will never be exactly the same. But if we really commit to this, it will have the almost tragi-comic consequence for his viewpoint that taking a number of prohibited substances off WADA's prohibited list could actually increase equality among competing athletes.

Again, I can conclude that, on reflection, an argument in favour of the current doping policy should not form the basis of punishing and stigmatising athletes like WADA does today.

Notes

1 For scholars discussing the view that doping is unfair, see, e.g. Douglas (2007), Lenk (2007) and Loland (2015).
2 Mølholm (2016).
3 WADA (2019).
4 WADA (2017).
5 See Savulescu, Foddy, and Clayton (2004, p. 669).
6 Ibid.
7 Booth et al. (1998).
8 See, e.g. Savulescu et al. (2004) regarding the price of EPO.
9 See, e.g. https://hypoxico.com/product/everest-summit-ii/ (accessed March 6, 2020).

7   Doping and onwards
Bottom of the ninth

Let's prepare the field and take stock of the results. So far, I have presented and criticised some of the most used and unavoidable arguments in favour of the current doping policy: That doping is unhealthy; that doping is contrary to the spirit of sport; that allowing doping would make children and young people start using doping; that athletes would feel coerced to use doping, was it allowed; that doping goes against the athletes' wishes and that doping prevents fair competition.

I have also shown that all these arguments are either based on wrong facts, unnecessarily vague concepts or double standards. I have, for instance, shown that allowing doping can in fact improve athlete health. And even in situations where doping might be unhealthy, we commonly allow athletes and non-athletes to do things and use substances (e.g. tobacco and alcohol) that are much more harmful than doping. So prohibiting doping just because it is unhealthy is either scientifically wrong or a double standard. I have further demonstrated that doping is also not contrary to the spirit of sport – quite the opposite – and that allowing doping can increase the autonomy of the athletes and actually increase the chances of fair competition.

However, the hopeful promoter of WADA's doping policy may point out that I have overlooked some of the key arguments in the debate. Arguments that have gone under my radar and have not been discussed in the preceding six chapters. So in the following, I will shortly present and critically discuss some of the arguments that are often not presented in the first line of defence when those making decisions in sport try to convince their audience of the wonders of the current doping rules. I hope that the following will make it crystal clear why these arguments are often kicked off the field and, in my opinion, should never play a role in the ethical debate on doping.

Doping is natural

That doping should be unnatural and therefore immoral is an argument that is sometimes used in the fight against legalised doping.[1] Let's call this the 'unnaturalness argument'. The unnaturalness argument can be used to defend the viewpoint that while it is immoral to inject EPO into your body with a syringe to increase the number of red blood cells, then it is morally acceptable to increase the number of red blood cells by means of altitude training or oxygen tents. So even if the effect is the same, you are allowed to believe that use of EPO is wrong because it is an unnatural way of increasing the number of red blood cells.

But it is far from clear, what it actually means, that an action is unnatural. However, I do not want to tire you with numerous definitions of what it means that an action is natural. The reason is simple; all the definitions I have seen are either idle talk (like: "Natural is good – but what is good? The natural is!") or they have extremely implausible implications if 'what is natural' is to serve as a moral compass in today's world.

In the most obvious definition of what it means for something to be natural, namely that the natural is in opposition to the cultural (the man-made), our current civilisation is primarily characterised by a long move away from the natural state or the natural. Without this move away from the natural, we would live like monkeys that run around naked in the forest or on the savannah. But if the most natural thing is to run around naked in the forest, and what is unnatural is immoral, then our ethical compass would be compromised, since almost everything would then be immoral.

Try asking yourself the following question: Is it natural when racing cyclists during time trials wear a skin suit and a long, aerodynamic helmet with integrated communication system and with frothing at the mouth ride on an insanely expensive bicycle – a bicycle fitted with disc wheels and time-trial bars? Supernatural? Hardly. Add to this that the rider's behind is greased up in chamois cream to allow him to glide effortlessly over the saddle – is that natural? You might very well think that the use of all this equipment and aids in prestigious races is unnatural. But why is that? I, for one, think that it is completely natural that humans compete and strive to become better by using the technology available. So I assume that it would also be fair to say that it is natural for humans to use a skin suit and disc wheels and all the other things needed to ride as fast as you can.

Moreover: Even if we manage to agree on what is unnatural, then it would still be important to answer the question of whether it is fair to infer from 'the unnatural' to the immoral. But that should not be the case. Simply because an action is branded as unnatural, it does not make sense to deem the action as immoral as well. If the unnatural is also immoral, then the use of the equipment and aids mentioned above would be an immoral act. I would think that very few people would find that using a skin suit, disc wheels or communication systems is immoral.

Doping ruins the attraction of sport

Another argument that is occasionally dusted off and used is that doping ruins the attraction of sport. Morten Mølholm, Director of the Sports Confederation of Denmark, is a proponent of this viewpoint:

> Doping is bad for sport, because doping violates the rules that have been made to protect the key attraction of sport: The transparent competition where nothing is given in advance.[2]

As I mentioned in the preceding chapter, athletes must observe the rules that apply in the sport they compete in. I also agree with Mølholm in so far as some of what makes sport exciting and entertaining is that the outcome is not given. Indeed, that is why we find match fixing in sport so immoral and destructive to the entertainment value. However, this observation from Mølholm is trite.

But it is not trite and actually quite strange that Mølholm in all seriousness believes that use of doping will remove one of the key attractions of sport, namely "… the transparent competition where nothing is given in advance". Is that really true? Would we really know in advance who would win if doping was allowed? I find that very hard to believe. If WADA removed all substances and methods from the prohibited list, it would not mean that we would know beforehand who would win a competition. If EPO was allowed – and everyone actually used EPO – then other factors would decide who would win a cycling race like Tour de France or a tennis tournament like Wimbledon. As stated in the previous chapter, such factors can include the athlete's genes and physique, the trainer's influence, the sport manager's planning skills, the athlete's tactical and technical skills, the right psychological mindset, etc. Or it might be a flat tyre and other accidents like the proverbial "black dog" or excited spectators who come in the way of the rider or player.[3] All these circumstances indicate that the outcome is not given in advance (whether the athletes dope or not).

Allow me to make up an example where the use of doping would indeed make it easy to predict the outcome of a match. Even if, for instance, the chefs Gordon Ramsay and Oliver Jamie took all the doping in the world, they would still not have a real chance of qualifying for the men's double at Wimbledon or the national tennis championships. In this situation, we would be able to predict who would win when someone uses doping. The chefs playing doubles would not stand a chance. So the argument that doping ruins one of the things that we find most attractive about elite sport – that the outcome is not given in advance – is utter nonsense.

Doping leads to a different game than sport

A third argument in the debate that I will attempt to shed some light on concludes that doping is immoral because it promotes a different game than sport. This argument would carry some weight if it was supported by the premise that doping is an immoral violation of the rules. However, the argument is also used to say that doping is inconsistent with participating in sport. But why is that? It seems very odd to claim that you cannot participate in sport if you dope. Assume that anabolic steroids were removed from the prohibited list and that football players use anabolic steroids to recover faster after an injury and to increase their muscle power. Would football then cease to exist? Hardly. In fact, it seems fair to assume that football would still exist. Only, the football players would add more muscle and be able to recover faster after an injury than they do today. I believe that the rules of football would probably roughly be the same except for the fact that the use of certain doping substances would be allowed.

It is naturally a possibility that a sport would change so dramatically that we would no longer refer to it as a sport, or that the sport in question would change so much that it lies so far away from what we think characterises a certain sport. If 100-metre runners had propellers on their back, we would probably stop calling it a 100-metre run; but that does not mean that it would be immoral to fly 100 metres, only that we would not allow propellers on the back of 100-metre runners. Yet, the same does not seem to apply to doping. In all the cases, I fail to find a good argument for the viewpoint that if you use doping in a certain sport, then you are not an athlete in this sport.

A pragmatic objection that could be made on the tail of the concern that doping will ruin the sport or change it beyond recognition would be to emphasise that there would be no spectators (or sponsors) for sport in which doping is used. But if some substances and methods were taken off WADA's prohibited list and therefore no longer would be prohibited to use, then we must assume that the outrage at the use of these substances would diminish considerably, since it would no longer constitute cheating. There is also something that indicates that the spectators and sponsors will continue to support sports and find it exciting and interesting to view sport when they know that doping is widespread among the athletes. To my knowledge, cycling has not lost much of its appeal in the wake of the doping scandals. The same applies to other sports like American football and tennis, which have also been struck by doping scandals.

Doping means that we cannot identify with the athlete

The final argument I will present, and which I have seen in the media, and discussed at seminars on sports ethics, concludes that doping is immoral because we as spectators are unable to identify with athletes who use doping.

But what is meant by a spectator identifying with an athlete in action is not quite clear. I'm not a psychologist, but allow be to make a homespun psychological explanation. When a spectator identifies with an athlete, I understand as much that the spectator recognises something in himself and his everyday life in what the athlete is doing in the sports arena. For instance, most will be able to identify with the athlete participating in a competition, because it is something we experience in our own life when we go to work, for example. Or we are able to identify with the fact that the athlete is sweating, because most of us know how it feels to sweat. Maybe not in connection with sport, but then on a hot summer's day, at the exam or on our first date.

But this argument has at least two flaws. First, it is not obvious that a sport activity is immoral simply because the spectator is unable to identify with the athlete. Being unable to identify with an athlete is probably something that many spectators can relate to. Sport can be an exciting past time to watch although we may not be able to see many similarities from our own life in what the athlete is doing. Although I often sat glued to the TV screen to watch Danish shot-putter and Olympic silver medallist Joachim B. Olsen perform at the beginning of this millennium, I did not identify with him. He lived, and lives, a life very different to mine. He weighs twice as much as I and is much stronger than I am, and I know practically nothing about shot-put. I'm just a pale academic working for the government (as does Joachim who is Member of Parliament for the Libertarian party, named Liberal Alliance) on a field outside Roskilde, who plays a bit of senior tennis in his spare time. Joachim B. Olsen is obviously a human like you and I, and I faintly identify with his successes and failures.

But what interested me in seeing Joachim in action with the heavy shots was mainly the excitement of seeing if he could win against some of the other strong athletes. Also, I enjoy watching something that has no resemblance with my everyday life. In 2017, I enjoyed and was in awe of Serena William's win at Australian Open, although I find it difficult to identify with Serena, who is a woman, American, has long hair, wears beautiful nail polish and was actually pregnant at the time. I experienced the same distance between spectator and athlete when my children were crazy with Lance Armstrong. But their lives had no resemblance with that of Armstrong. There was nothing strange in that. Few people would be able to identify with a person who trains as much and rides as fast as Lance did at the pinnacle of his career. But that does not make it immoral that Joachim, Lance and Serena competed at a level that most of us are unable to comprehend and identify with. The same lack of identification between spectators and athletes can be seen in football. Fanatic football fans have often very little in common with the players on the team they support other than wanting the team to win. When we talk about identification in the world of sports, it would perhaps be more reasonable to talk about the players identifying with each other or the spectators identifying with each other.

Second: In the cases where a spectator actually identifies with an athlete, why would he not be able to identify with an athlete who uses doping. If the spectator uses doping, doping among athletes and spectators might increase the identification between spectator and athlete. "We are both doing something to optimise our experience, we use what is needed of alcohol and pills, it's all the same" might be one way a spectator watching a doped athlete going full throttle on the field, ice rink or tennis court would argue.

It is clear why the arguments dealt with in this chapter do not constitute the first line of defence in favour of a doping policy. Broadly speaking, and as I have argued, doping is not unnatural as it is part of human nature to use the technology available to get what we want. And if doping is unnatural – and therefore immoral – then we should also find it immoral if a racing cyclist uses a skin suit, disc wheels and chamois creame. Furthermore, it seems odd that doping should threaten the attraction of sport; the fact that the outcome is not given. As Danish cartoonist Storm P put it: "It's difficult to predict, especially about the future". The same would apply if all athletes used doping. We would not know who would win the Tour de France or at the Olympic Games, even if doping was allowed. We have seen this in

Tour de France history. Because even though many tour riders have been or are doped, you do not know who will win the race *before* it starts.

That doping would result in a different game than sport is also hard to fathom. Using doping and making doping substances legal are fully consistent with competing in sport as we know it today. Again, history is on our side. That Bjarne Riis and Lance Armstrong did not participate in a sport like cycling because they were doped sounds like a problematic claim. What then were they doing when they rode around the Alps during the Tour de France? Looking at birds or just messing around!? No, they were naturally part of a race, just like the other riders in the peloton. That doping should make the spectators unable to identify with the doped athletes is nonsense, if you think about it. Identifying with an athlete in the sense that you have something special in common with the athlete is not at all necessary. As spectators we are perfectly able to enjoy and get excited about watching sport without having to identify particularly with the athlete.

I love watching animal movies and watch and try to understand why a beaver builds a dam. That is no problem and is hardly immoral although I do not identify strongly with the beaver. However, if you identify strongly with a beaver when you watch one in nature or on TV, then maybe you also build dams or have large incisors – so what? So again, and drawing on the example with the beaver, lack of identification between a spectator and an athlete should not be an indication of whether doping is morally wrong.

Notes

1 For a more in debt discussion of the idea that doping is unnatural, see, e.g. Miah (2004).
2 Hansen (2003).
3 I will spare you a detailed description of the incident where a highly intoxicated Danish spectator ran onto the field during a football game between Sweden and Denmark in 2007 and threw a punch at the referee. The result of this incident was, among other things, that Denmark lost the three goals it had scored and therefore lost the match.

References

Abel, E. L. (2007). Football increases the risk for Lou Gehrig's disease, amyotrophic lateral sclerosis. *Perceptual and Motor Skills, 104*(3_suppl), 1251–1254.

Abbott, A. (2000). What price the Olympian ideal? *Nature, 407*, 124–127.

Bailey, D. M., Robach, P., Thomsen, J. J., & Lundby, C. (2006). Erythropoietin depletes iron stores: Antioxidant neuroprotection for ischemic stroke? *Stroke, 37*(10), 2453–2453.

Beamish, R. (2009). Steroids, symbolism and morality: The construction of a social problem and its unintended consequences. In Møller, V., McNamee, M., & Dimeo, P. (Eds.) *Elite sport, doping and public health* (pp. 55–73). Odense: University of Southern Denmark.

Binmore, K. (2007). *Game theory: A very short introduction.* Oxford: Oxford University Press.

Booth, F. W. et al. (1998). Molecular and cellular adaption of muscle in response to physical training. *Acta Physiology Scandinavia, 162*(3), 343–350.

Bostrom, N., & Roache, R. (2008). Ethical issues in human enhancement. In Ryberg, J., Petersen, T. S., & Wolff, C. (Eds.) *New waves in applied ethics* (pp. 120–152). New York: Palgrave MacMillian.

Breivik, G. (1987). The doping dilemma: Some game theoretical and philosophical considerations. *Sportswissenschaft, 17*(1), 83–94.

Brown, W. J., Basil, M. D., & Bocarnea, M. C. (2003). The influence of famous athletes on health beliefs and practices: Mark McGwire, child abuse prevention, and androstenedione. *Journal of Health Communication, 8*(1), 41–57.

Chomiak, J., Junge, A., Peterson, L., & Dvorak, J. (2016). Severe injuries in football players. *The American Journal of Sports Medicine, 28*(5), 58–68.

Coyle, D. (2005). *Lance Armstrong: Tour De Force.* New York: Harper Collins Publishers.

Douglas, T. (2007). Enhancement in sport, and enhancement outside sport. *Studies in Ethics, Law, and Technology, 1*(1). https://www.degruyter.com/view/journals/selt/1/1/selt.1.issue-1.xml

Dimeo, P., & Møller, W. (2018). *The anti-doping crisis in sport.* London: Routledge.

Donati, A. (2007). World traffic in doping substances. https://www.wada-ama.org/sites/default/files/resources/files/WADA_Donati_Report_On_Trafficking_2007.pdf

Eichner, E. R. (2007). Blood doping. *Sports Medicine, 37*(4–5), 389–391.

Fraleigh, W. P. (1985). Performance-enhancing drug in sport: The ethical issue. *Journal of the Philosophy of Sport, 11*(1), 33–35.

Hansen, M. M. (2003). Doping truer sportens væsentligste attraktion. *Politiken* (Danish newspaper), July 28.

Hartgens, F., & Kuipers, H. (2004). Effects of androgenic-anabolic steroids in athletes. *Sports Medicine, 34*(8), 513–554.

Hass, U., & Healey, D. (Eds.) (2016). *Doping in sport and the law.* Oxford: Hart Publishing.

Holowchak, A. (2000). "Aretism" and pharmacological ergogenic aids in sport: Taking a shot at the use of steroids. *Journal of the Philosophy of Sport, 27*(1), 35–50.

Hood, A. (2017). How many times was Armstrong tested? *Velonews*, January 23.

Hunt, T. M. (2011). *Drug games: The International Olympic Committee and the politics of doping, 1960–2008.* Austin: University of Texas Press.

Johnson, M. (2016). *Spitting in the soup: Inside the dirty game of doping in sports.* Boulder: VeloPress.

Kayser, B. E. (2009). Current anti-doping policy: Harm reduction or harm induction? *The ethics of doping and anti-doping: Redeeming the soul of sport?* In V. Møller, M. J. McNamee & P. Dimeo (Eds.), *Elite sport, doping, and public health* (pp. 155–165). Odense: University Press of Southern Denmark.

Kious, B. M. (2008). Philosophy on steroids: Why the anti-doping position could use a little enhancement. *Theoretical Medicine and Bioethics, 29*(4), 213–234.

Lenk, C. (2007). Is enhancement in sport really unfair? Arguments on the concept of competition and equality of opportunities. *Sports, Ethics and Philosophy, 1*(2), 218–228.

Loland, S. (2015). Fair play. In McNamee, M., & Morgan, W. J. (Eds.), *Routledge handbook of the philosophy of sport* (pp. 333–350). London: Routledge.

López, B. (2011). The invention of a 'drug of mass destruction': Deconstructing the EPO myth. *Sport in History, 31*(1), 84–109.

Lundby, C., & Olsen, N. V. (2011). Effects of recombinant human erythropoietin in normal humans. *The Journal of Physiology, 589*(6), 1265–1271.

Mazanov, J. (2016). *Managing drugs in sport.* London: Routledge.

McNamee, M. J. (2012). The spirit of sport and the medicalisation of anti-doping: Empirical and normative ethics. *Asian Bioethics Review, 4*(4), 374–392.

Miah, A. (2004). *Genetically modified athletes: Biomedical ethics, gene doping and sport.* London: Routledge.

Mikkelsen, B. (2003). Doping demands action now! Ekstra Bladet (Danish newspaper), March 1.

Miller, K. E., Barnes, G. M., Sabo, D., Melnick, M. J., & Farrell, M. P. (2002). A comparison of health risk behavior in adolescent users of anabolic-androgenic steroids, by gender and athlete status. *Sociology of Sport Journal, 19*(4), 385–402.

Mølholm, M. (2016). Derfor skal doping bekæmpes. *Jyllands-Posten* (Danish newspaper). December 29. https://www.dif.dk/da/politik/nyheder/nyheder/2016/december/20161228_doping (Accessed February 5, 2020).

Møller, V. (2010). *The ethics of doping and anti-doping.* London: Routledge.

Mueller, F., & Colgate, B. (2013). *Annual survey of football injury research: 1931–2012.* Chapel Hill: National Center for Catastrophic Sport Injury Research, University of North Carolina at Chapel Hill.

Murray, T. H. (1983). The coercive power of drugs in sports. *Hastings Center Report, 13*(4), 24–30.

Ninot, G., Connes, P., & Caillaud, C. (2006). Effects of recombinant human erythropoietin injections on physical self in endurance athletes. *Journal of Sports Sciences, 24*(4), 383–391.

Nozick, R. (1969). Coercion. In S. Morgenbesser (ed.), *Philosophy, science, and method* (pp. 440–472). London: Macmillan.

Paoli, L., & Donati, A. (2013). *The sports doping market: Understanding supply and demand and the challenges of their control.* New York: Springer.

Petersen, T. S. (2010). Good athlete – Bad athlete? On the 'role-model argument' for banning performance-enhancing drugs. *Sport, Ethics and Philosophy, 4*(3), 332–340.

Petersen, T. S., & Kristensen, J. (2009). Should athletes be allowed to use all kinds of performance-enhancing drugs? – A critical note on Claudio Tamburrini. *Journal of the Philosophy of Sport, 36*(1), 88–98.

Petersen, T. S., & Lippert-Rasmussen, K. (2007). Prohibiting drugs in sports: An enhanced proposal. In J. Ryberg, T. S. Petersen & C. Wolf (red.), *New waves in applied ethics* (pp. 237–260). Basingstoke: Palgrave Macmillan.

Petersen, T. S., & Lopez Frias, F. J. (2020). Promoting fairness in sport through performance-enhancing substances: An argument for why sport referees ought to 'Be on Drugs'. *Sport, Ethics and Philosophy,* 1–9 (online first).

Pitsch, W., & Emrich, E. (2012). The frequency of doping in elite sport: Results of a replication study. *International Review for the Sociology of Sport, 47*(5), 559–580.

Pound, R. W. (2006). *Inside dope: How drugs are the biggest threat to sports, why you should care, and what can be done about them.* Missisauga: Wiley & Sons.

Pryor, J., Larson, A., & DeBeliso, M. (2016). The prevalence of depression and concussions in a sample of active North American semi-professional and professional football players. *Journal of Lifestyle Medicine, 6*(1), 7.

Rasmussen, M., & Wivel, K. (2013). *Gul feber (yellow fever).* København: People's Press. (In Danish).

Rough, P. (2005): Bode Miller's take on doping in alpine skiing: Legalize it? *Skiracing.* October 2.

Savulescu, J., & Foddy, B. (2011). Le tour and failure of zero tolerance: Time to relax doping controls. In Savulescu, J., Meulen, R., & Kahane, G. (Eds.), *Enhancing human capacities* (pp. 304–312). New Jersey: Blackwell Publishing.

Savulescu, J., Foddy, B., & Clayton, M. (2004). Why we should allow performance enhancing drugs in sport. *British Journal of Sports Medicine, 38*(6), 666–670.

Tamburrini, C. M. (2000). What's wrong with doping? In T. Tännsjö & C. Tamburrini (Eds.), *Values in Sport* (pp. 200–216). London: E & FN Spon.

Tamburrini, C. M., & Tännsjö, T. (Ed.) (2005). *Genetic technology and sport: Ethical questions.* London: Routledge.

UK Department for Digital, Culture, Media & Sport (2017). Review of Criminalization of Doping in Sport. Policy Paper: https://www.gov.uk/government/publications/review-of-criminalisation-of-doping-in-sport (Accessed June 3, 2020).

Ulrich, R., Pope, H. G., & Cléret, L. et al. (2018). Doping in two elite athletics competitions assessed by randomized-response surveys. *Sports Medicine, 48*(1), 211–219.

Veber, M. (2014). The coercion argument against performance-enhancing drugs. *Journal of the Philosophy of Sport, 41*(2), 267–277.

WADA (2019). *World anti-doping code 2015: With 2019 amendements.* Montreal: World Anti-Doping Agency. https://www.wada-ama.org/en/resources/the-code/world-anti-doping-code (Assessed June 3, 2020).

WADA (2020). *2020 list of prohibited substances and methods.* Montreal: World Anti-Doping Agency. https://www.wada-ama.org/en/content/what-is-prohibited (Accessed June 3, 2020).

WADA Ethics Panel (2017). https://www.wada-ama.org/en/resources/the-code/2021-world-anti-doping-code (Accessed June 3, 2020).

WADA Leflet (2020). Dangers of doping: Get the facts. https://www.wada-ama.org/sites/default/files/resources/files/WADA_Dangers_of_Doping_EN.pdf (Assessed June 3, 2020).

Waldén, M., Hägglund, M., & Ekstrand, J. (2007). Football injuries during European championships 2004–2005. *Knee Surgery, Sports Traumatology Arthroscopy, 15*(9), 1155–1162.

Index

Note: Page numbers followed by 'n' refer to end notes